TRANSLATION QUALITY ASSESSMENT

PERSPECTIVES ON TRANSLATION SERIES

The Perspectives on Translation series consists of works that analyze translation from a theoretical or practical point of view. In addition to the history, methodology, and theory, the series covers lexicology, terminology, interpretation... Textbooks for students as well as for professional translators and interpreters can be found in the Didactics of Translation series. Both series welcome manuscripts written in either English or French.

In the same series:

Renate Blumenfeld-Kosinski, Luise von Flotow and Daniel Russell (eds.), *The Politics of Translation in the Middle Ages and the Renaissance*, 2001.

Sherry Simon and Paul St-Pierre (eds.), *Changing Terms: Translating in the Postcolonial Era*, 2000.

Ruth A. Roland, *Interpreters as Diplomats: A Diplomatic History of the Role of Interpreters in World Politics*, 1999.

Francesca Gaiba (ed.), *The Origins of Simultaneous Interpretation: The Nuremberg Trial*, 1988.

In the Didactics of Translation series:

Lynne Bowker, *Computer-Aided Translation Technology: A Practical Introduction*, 2002.

Allison Beeby Lonsdale, *Teaching Translation from Spanish to English. Worlds beyond Words*, 1996.

PERSPECTIVES ON TRANSLATION

Series Director: Jean Delisle

TRANSLATION QUALITY ASSESSMENT:

An Argumentation-Centred Approach

Malcolm Williams

University of Ottawa Press

Library and Archives Canada Cataloguing in Publication

Williams, Malcolm, 1946-
Translation quality assessment: an argumentation-centred approach / Malcolm Williams.

(Perspectives on translation)
Includes bibliographical references and index.
ISBN 0-7766-0584-4

1. Translating and interpreting—Evaluation. I. Title. II. Series.

P306.2.W54 2004 418'.02 C2004-904313-7

University of Ottawa Press gratefully acknowledges the support extended to its publishing program by the Canada Council and the University of Ottawa.

We acknowledge the financial support of the Government of Canada through the Book Publishing Industry Development Program (BPIDP) for our publishing activities.

Copy-editing: Käthe Roth
Proofreading: Laurel Hyatt
Typesetting: Brad Horning

ISBN 0-7766-0584-4
ISSN 1480-7734

542 King Edward Avenue, Ottawa, Ont. Canada K1N 6N5

press@uottawa.ca http://www.uopress.uottawa.ca

Printed and bound in Canada

*Dedicated to my family—Christine, Marc,
Christopher, Matthew, and Julia—for their support
(and patience!)*

CONTENTS

ACKNOWLEDGMENTS

I owe a considerable debt of gratitude to Annie Brisset, University of Ottawa, for sparking my interest in argumentation theory and giving me enthusiastic support and guidance during the writing of the thesis that was the starting point for this book.

Thanks also go to Roda Roberts, University of Ottawa, for encouraging me to embark on translation studies in the first place and for giving me invaluable advice on preparing my thesis for publication, and to Jean Delisle, director of the University of Ottawa School of Translation and Interpretation, for his encouragement and counsel.

Finally, I would like to express my appreciation to Gaston St-Jean of the Canadian Criminal Justice Association, Jacqueline Elton of the Ontario Government Translation Services, the Centre for Data and Analysis on Transportation, and the Office of Energy Efficiency of Natural Resources Canada for providing me with the material on which the argumentation-centred translation quality assessment model was tested.

MALCOLM WILLIAMS
Ottawa
November 2003

INTRODUCTION

> The assessment of translator performance is an activity which, despite being widespread, is under-researched and under-discussed.
>
> (Hatim and Mason 1997)

Translation quality assessment (TQA) is not a new field of inquiry. Moreover, it has the distinction of being one that interests a broad range of practitioners, researchers, and organizations, whether their focus is literary or instrumental (pragmatic) translation. Concern for excellence in translation or literary and religious works dates back centuries. Quality in instrumental translation as a subject of discussion is a more recent phenomenon, but as far back as 1959, at an international conference of the Fédération Internationale des Traducteurs on quality in Paris, E. Cary and others were already debating the requirements of a good translation. More recently still, with the advent of globalization, the coming of age of translation as part of the language industries, and the concomitant emphasis on "total quality" and ISO certification in private industry in general, special issues of *Circuit* (1994) and *Language International* (1998) have been devoted to quality-assurance processes, professional standards, and accreditation; Austrian, German, and Italian standardization organizations have issued national translation standards; and a European standard is scheduled for approval in 2005.

The reasons for the interest in quality and TQA have, of course, evolved: where they were once primarily aesthetic, religious, and political, they are now primarily pedagogical, administrative (e.g., evaluation of students), and economic and legal (e.g., pre-delivery quality control/assurance; post-delivery evaluation to ensure that terms of contract have been met by supplier). Hönig spells out why various groups need TQA:

> *Users* need it because they want to know whether they can trust the translators and rely on the quality of their products.

> *Professional translators* need it because there are so many amateur translators who work for very little money that professional translators will only be able to sell their products if there is some proof of the superior quality of their work.
>
> *Translatological research* needs it because if it does not want to become academic and marginal in the eyes of practising translators it must establish criteria for quality control and assessment.
>
> *Trainee translators* need it because otherwise they will not know how to systematically improve the quality of their work. (1998: 15)

In short, the relevance of, and justification for, TQA is stronger than ever. Yet whereas there is general agreement on the requirement for a translation to be "good," "satisfactory," or "acceptable," the definition of acceptability and of the means of determining it are matters of ongoing debate and there is precious little agreement on specifics. National translation standards may exist, but, as the organizers of a 1999 conference on translation quality in Leipzig, the Institut für Angewandte Linguistik und Translatologie, noted, no generally accepted objective criteria currently exist for evaluating the quality of translations. Even the national and international standards, DIN 2345 and the ISO-9000 series, do not provide for evaluation of translation quality in specific contexts. The result is assessment chaos.

What are the problems and issues that stand in the way of consensus and coherence in TQA? What do practitioners and theorists disagree about?

First, many TQA models have been developed with literary, advertising, and journalistic translation in mind. The principles underlying them do not necessarily apply to other types of instrumental translation. Furthermore, the focus of the designers of a number of models has been on highlighting cultural differences reflected in translations and on showing how high-quality translation may be "literal" or "free," depending on the cultural and linguistic constraints involved. Discussion of errors caused by other factors (inadequate linguistic or encyclopedic knowledge, failure to use context) is overshadowed by the designers' interest in cultural issues of translation.

Second, people disagree on whether, or to what extent, factors extraneous to the "absolute" quality of the translation—deadline, difficulty of source text, end use, competence of evaluator, etc.—should affect the "absolute" assessment. In addition, the more criteria, or variables, that are incorporated into the measurement grid and process in order to "make allowances," the more complex the model and process are likely to become.

Third, whose notion of quality should take precedence? The translation service's notion of quality may not match the requirements of the client/end user/reader, particularly regarding style, vocabulary, and level of language. For example, the use of standard French, or "le français universel," might well be considered inappropriate in a text for technicians with the Canadian Armed Forces, yet the standard-language translation could still be rated satisfactory in vacuo, without consideration for the end user's sociolect.

Fourth, perhaps the most contentious issue in TQA is the lack of uniformity in assessment of language errors. Elegant style is considered essential by some evaluators, but not by others. Some evaluators consider typos and spelling and punctuation errors to be peccadilloes and ignore them in their overall assessment, while others regard them as serious because they are precisely the errors that the client/end user will detect.

The issue of the standard written language is relevant here too. A cursory perusal of recent issues of leading journals on the English language suffices to show how writing about the problem of standard spoken English has become an industry in itself. Yet, on the matter of the written language, a contributor to a recent issue of *English Today* concluded that guides to good writing "did not address the question of an international written standard English" (Gaskell 2000: 49). So if the standard is unstable, the assessment of language error in an era of trade globalization and internationalization of the English language becomes a risky exercise.

Fifth, the same inconsistency is apparent in the assessment of level of accuracy. Some evaluators will ignore minor shifts in meaning if the core message is preserved in the translation, while others will insist on total "fidelity," even if the omission of a concept at one point is offset by its inclusion elsewhere in the text.

Sixth, TQA has traditionally been based on intensive error detection and analysis and has therefore required a considerable investment in human resources. It takes time. One means of obviating the problem has been sampling—the analysis of samples of translations rather than of whole texts. However, this approach has shortcomings, not the least of which is the fact that serious errors committed outside the samples will remain undetected.

Seventh, TQA is more often than not based on quantification of error. Microtextual analysis of samples has been used extensively not only because it saves time but also because it provides error counts as a justification for a negative assessment. Translation services and teachers of translation alike have developed TQA grids with several quality levels, or grades, based on the number of errors in a short text. It is felt that quantification lends objectivity to the assessment. The problem lies with the borderline cases. Assuming that, in order to be user-friendly, such a grid does not allow for many levels of seriousness of error, it is quite possible for a translation containing one more error than the maximum allowed to be as good as, if not better than, another translation with exactly the maximum number of errors allowed and yet be rated unsatisfactory.

Eighth, one way to circumvent the drawbacks of quantification is to grade errors by seriousness: critical/major, minor, weakness, and so on. The problem, then, is to seek a consensus on what constitutes a major, as opposed to a minor, error. For example, an error in translating numerals may be considered critical by some, particularly in financial, scientific, or technical material, yet others will claim that the client or end user will recognize the slip-up and automatically correct it in the process of reading.

Ninth, Darbelnet (1977: 16) identifies no fewer than nine levels, or parameters, at or against which the quality of a translation should be assessed: accuracy of individual translation units; accuracy of translation as a whole; idiomaticity; correctness of target language; tone; cultural differences; literary and other artistic allusions; implicit intentions of author; and adaptation to end user. Other models provide for an assessment of level of accuracy, target language quality, and format (appearance of text). The problem is this: Assuming that one can make a fair assessment of each parameter, how does one then generate an overall quality rating for the translation?

Finally, within the industry itself, the characteristics of a scheme designed to assure quality before delivery to the customer may be different from one developed for cyclical quality audits by a central auditing agency. Within training institutions, the characteristics of a TQA scheme may vary depending on whether the purpose is formative assessment (to provide feedback in support of the learning process) or summative evaluation (to provide evidence of translation competence in order for a student to be awarded certification, pass a course, etc.).

Clearly, "the devil is in the details." It is not surprising that it has proved impossible to establish a quality standard that meets all requirements and can be used to assess specific translations. Hence, DIN 2345 follows in the footsteps of the ISO 9000 series, erring on the side of caution in its proposed guidelines for quality control. It does not establish a standard of acceptability or levels of quality, nor does it provide a TQA tool. The search for translation quality standards and measurement tools modelled on ISO quality standards and methods of industrial quality control is a worthwhile endeavour because it responds to the need for objectivity (through precise measurement and quantification) and for instruments that will enjoy widespread approval. However, a translation is an intellectual product and, as such, is a complex, heterogeneous one, not a physical unit that can be replicated exactly by a machine thousands of times. This is why TQA has proven to be so difficult and why TQA models have so many detractors.

The problems are legion. My purpose here is not to attempt to resolve them all. My main goal is to propose solutions to the problems of sampling, quantification and borderline cases, type of error, and the level of seriousness of error. The TQA models that have actually been put into practice in the translation industry are microtextual: they tend to focus on discrete lexical and morphosyntactic units at the subsentence level and to be applied to short passages of texts. While this does not prevent the evaluator from detecting shortcomings and strong points in that text, microtextual models are not designed to assess each passage as an integral part of a whole, to take account of the fact that the translation of the short passage is, in principle at least, determined in part by, and in its turn influences, the text as a whole, or to evaluate the logic and coherence existing even within the sample passage itself. A number of researchers, including House and Larose, have proposed elements of discourse analysis as a means of bridging the gap between, on the one hand, the microtextual approach of professional TQA systems and, on the other hand, the theoretical and practical need to enhance TQA validity and reliability (consistency in TQA results) by integrating a macrotextual, discourse (textological or text-linguistic) perspective, along with relevant aspects of pragmatics, into the assessment process. However, models of this type have not been fully developed and tested on instrumental translations; they have generally been applied to journalistic and literary documents in a student-training context.

Accordingly, I explore the application of one particular aspect of discourse analysis—argumentation theory—to TQA and develop an assessment framework to complement existing microtextual schemes, with specific reference to instrumental translation in a production context. I will exploit the following aspects of argumentation theory: overall argument structure (superstructure) of the text, propositional functions, conjunctives and inference indicators, types of argument, figures of speech, and narrative strategy. In so doing, I will show that assessing transfer of argument necessarily leads to an examination of the macrotext, of the messages conveyed in the text, and of the reasoning on which they are based.

In addition, I will show how the application of argumentation theory to TQA can serve to remove some of the subjectivity and randomness from decisions on the acceptability of translations. As stated above, the challenge of setting and defining levels of acceptable and unacceptable quality and determining the acceptability threshold—the level of tolerance of errors—is a daunting one. Whatever criteria and factors quality is judged against, TQA models can generally demonstrate convincingly that a translation is very good or very bad. However, the hardest, and perhaps the most interesting, part of the evaluator's task is deciding on the borderline cases, because a grade based only on the number of errors may not be a fair reflection of translation quality. In an effort to resolve this issue, I will focus on the relationship between level of seriousness of error and full-text analysis, using argumentation theory to determine what is important in the messages conveyed by the text and defining "major error" accordingly.

Finally, the definition of acceptability threshold leads us to that of the translation quality standard itself. Only recently has there been any discussion in translation studies of what exactly translation quality standards are. For example, Nord and Chesterman have developed a concept of translation "norms" on the basis of theories of linguistic and social norms proposed by linguists and philosophers. But how does the broad concept of a translation norm fit in with the more practical features of a TQA scheme? Does the current mantra of "zero defects" suffice to constitute our quality standard? Or can discourse analysis provide us with a more precise standard without exposing us to the perils of quantification? What is the basis for, and what are the characteristics of, a translation quality standard? These are important questions, particularly since the development of translation as an industry has legal ramifications such as financial penalties for nonperformance of contracts and disqualification of translators. On the basis of the argumentation-centred model to be developed and the results of testing that model, I will then propose a discourse-based (textological) translation quality standard.

I hasten to add that, in analyzing and judging translations, I will not be broaching the philosophical problems of meaning, interpretation, fidelity, adequacy, and acceptability explored by Ricoeur, Eco, Nanni, Bourdieu, Toury, and others. I will develop and demonstrate my model with reference to instrumental translations produced in an institutional context, and my approach is predicated on the possibility and necessity of accuracy and of a translation that reads as though it was in fact originated in the target language.

The function of the planned assessment model will be summative, not formative: it will serve primarily to assess the quality of product and thereby translator competence for administrative purposes. Use of the model for formative assessment and training will be the focus of a future study.

Two appendixes have been included. The first contains a model assessment, showing the reader how the grids developed in the book are used and combined in a specific case. The second presents definitions of TQA-related terms and terms specific to argumentation theory. Terms used in the book that are defined in the appendix are boldfaced at first mention in the chapters that follow.

PART I

DEVELOPING AN ARGUMENTATION-CENTRED TQA MODEL

CHAPTER ONE

THE PRESENT STATE OF TQA AND STUDY OBJECTIVES

1.1. TQA approaches

Below, I summarize and compare a number of important TQA models. Whether they have actually been put into practice or have merely been proposed, almost all have one feature in common: categorization of errors lies at the heart of each approach. That being said, their concept of categorization differs, according to (1) whether or not they incorporate quantitative **measurement** and (2) whether they are **standards-referenced** (based on fixed **standards** that have to be met) or **criterion-referenced** (based on specific objectives that have to be achieved for a given **text**), and they can be classified on that basis.

1.1.1. Models with a quantitative dimension

Canadian Language Quality Measurement System (Sical)
The TQA model developed by the Canadian government's Translation Bureau is the best-known one, at least on the Canadian scene. It was developed both as an examination tool and to help the Bureau assess the **quality** of the 300 million words of **instrumental translation** that it delivered yearly. Applied from 1986 to 1994, the third-generation Sical incorporated a scheme based on the quantification of errors and on a twofold distinction between (1) translation (transfer) and **language errors** and (2) major and minor errors. Texts were given quality ratings according to the number of major and minor errors in a 400-word passage: A—superior (0 major errors/maximum of 6 minor); B—fully acceptable (0/12); C—revisable (1/18); and D—unacceptable. As such, it was a standards-referenced model: quality levels were defined in terms of the errors that a text of a given standard could contain.

The major error was defined as follows:

> Translation: Complete failure to render the meaning of a word or passage that contains an essential element of the message; also, mistranslation resulting in a contradiction of or significant departure from the meaning of an essential element of the message.
>
> Language: Incomprehensible, grossly incorrect language or rudimentary error in an essential element of the message. (Williams 1989: 26)

The key word is *essential*. It was left up to the quality controller or evaluator to determine whether an essential element of the message was at issue.

The typology of errors established in this context—a typology modelled on that of Horguelin (1978)—is indicative of the fact that the quality system by and large focused on the word and the sentence, not on the text as a whole. Larose sums up the approach as follows:

> The Sical grid is based mainly on the syntactic and semantic aspects of the text, not on its discursive dimension, which lies beyond the statement and between statements. (Larose 1998: 175; our translation)

For the purpose of assessing the quality of professional translators' work before delivery to the client (**quality assurance** or **control**) or after (**evaluation**), quality controllers and evaluators were required to select one or more representative 400-word samples of texts. Thus the essential or nonessential nature of a word or passage was necessarily determined on the basis of the word or sample, not the text as a whole.

The year 1994 signalled a major shift in the Translation Bureau's approach to TQA. Implicit in the application of Sical and the quantification of errors was recognition of the fact that translations assessed as deliverable contained errors—officially as many as 12. Since the Bureau was to enter into direct competition with the private sector in 1995, management concluded that a "total quality" approach was necessary. Thenceforth "zero **defects**" was the order of the day: the Bureau was committed to delivering error-free translations to its clients. There was no longer any question of a tolerance threshold and of determining whether that threshold had been crossed in one or more samples. The quality of work is no longer simply vetted by means of sampling; the quality controller's approach to a translation can range from no assessment at all to a comparative examination, and revision, of the text in its entirety.

At time of writing, fixed grids are used only for the marking of recruitment examinations and the **assessment** of interns' translations (under a partnership program between the Bureau and Canadian schools of translation). In the case of examinations, a modified Sical has been devised in which the major error is worth three minor errors for calculation purposes. The length of the examination text can vary.

In short, the microtextual approach to TQA remains, but no single, quantifiable standard, or range of tolerance levels, is applied and sampling is no longer done automatically. The approach is very much tailored to specific conditions.

Council of Translators and Interpreters of Canada (CTIC)

Sical has influenced a number of Canadian models, including that of the CTIC. The Council uses a comparable standards-referenced model for its translator certification examinations, except that "no single repeated error will be considered sufficient to fail a candidate" (CTIC 2001: 2.2). Each type of error in the candidate's paper is given a quantitative value (–10, –5, –3) and the total of these values is subtracted from 100: the candidate with an average of 70% or higher in two translations of about 175 words each passes. Unlike Sical, the definition of major and minor error does not relate error to an essential part of the message:

> Translation (comprehension)
>
> Major mistakes, e.g., serious mistranslation denoting a definite lack in comprehension of the **source language**, nonsense, omission of a phrase or more
>
> Language (expression)
>
> Major mistakes, e.g., gibberish, unacceptable structure

Thus it is fair to say that the definition of "major error" under both Sical and CTIC leaves considerable room for judgment and, some would contend, subjectivity on the part of the evaluator.

Ontario Government Translation Services (GTS)

GTS revised its quality assessment procedures in 2000. The Ontario government contracts out most of its translation work, and contractors' drafts are assessed by a group of experienced in-house translators (called co-ordinators) before delivery to the client ministries and agencies. Their assessments are used to give clients an indication of the quality of individual translations and of any need for revision, as well as to update a database on contractor performance.

The revised procedures are purportedly based on Sical. They do, however, present some interesting differences from the Translation Bureau model. First, the evaluator is required to read through the whole **target text** to identify potential problems before selecting any samples.

Second, the evaluator must identify errors and make separate "overall assessments" of "quality of translation" and "quality of language used, style of text" without reference to **context**, in order to assess the usability of the translation. Judgment of usability is based not on a fixed quantitative standard but on a "guideline" for errors of transfer: a short text containing a 400-word sample with more than 5 minor errors or 1 major error could be considered unusable without revision. A major **translation error** is defined as one that seriously impedes the main message. However, no definition of "seriously impede" or "main message" is offered—it is presumably left to the co-ordinator's discretion.

Third, the evaluator must determine whether the delivery deadline was met and assess quality of layout and appearance before making a combined overall assessment covering all four factors (transfer, language, deadline, and layout/appearance) and taking the context into account. In other words, a relative quality **rating** follows the absolute quality rating. In establishing the rating, the co-ordinator is to consider a number of external factors: tight deadline (inability to check terminology and clarify problems), highly technical text (limited number of suppliers, limited circulation), background material and/or contact person unavailable, length and purpose of text, target readership, and end use (publication, internal distribution) (Ontario Government Translation Services 2000: 3).

Again, much is left to the discretion and experience of the co-ordinator/evaluator—for example, how to determine usability notwithstanding errors and how to pool the four overall assessments (of translation, language quality, meeting the deadline, and layout) into one. In addition, there is no explanation for the approximate quantitative value of the "usable" text (no more than 5 minor errors/1 major translation error) and no clear indication as to whether the same value also applies to language errors. Thus, while error categorization and the quantitative guideline echo Sical, the GTS model is not so much standards-referenced as criterion-referenced, depending on the evaluator's weighting of the various characteristics of the texts and the external factors at play. That being said, the requirement for overall assessment, based not only on linguistic but also on other factors, is explicitly stated, whereas in the Translation Bureau model it is not.

Système d'évaluation positive des traductions (SEPT)
SEPT was developed for the Translation Bureau by Daniel Gouadec in the late seventies, but it was never put into practice, probably because of its complexity: SEPT is based on 675 parameters, requiring a great number of linguistic and statistical operations and judgments on the part of the evaluator.

SEPT is complex because it is perhaps the most comprehensive TQA model devised to date. For example, it is designed to take the level of difficulty of the **source text** and any particularly good translation solutions into account in establishing the quality level of the translation and to ensure the objectivity of the TQA process even more firmly than Sical. "Instead of the evaluator having to determine the seriousness of errors each time," writes Gouadec, "the system has to do it" (1989: 3; our translation). His aim is to provide a "neutral" system that would control ("prendre en charge") the evaluator and, through linguistic analysis and statistics, determine the source, nature, and effect of each error.

Unlike the other models, SEPT is predicated on an explicit recognition that errors can be microtextual and/or macrotextual: they can be linguistic (formal), semantic (affecting the sentence), and contextual (affecting the content of the text). Through identification and weighting of translation units, Gouadec incorporates into his system a measurement of the degree of difficulty of the source text, which evaluators take into consideration in rating the target text. A specific number of "penalty" points is assessed for each type of error, and the total number of points is subtracted from 100 to give an initial percentage score, which may be revised upward following another set of calculations reflecting source text difficulty and bonus points for strong points in the translation.

More recently, Gouadec has suggested a simpler approach than SEPT. His proposed grid is based on three levels of acceptable quality: publishable (zero defects); deliverable (full accuracy for information purposes); and revisable (some weaknesses in transfer of meaning and terminology). These levels are comparable to the Sical III quality levels A, B and C, except that no specific number of errors is assigned to a level. Indeed, it is unlikely that Gouadec's notion of "full accuracy" would extend to the 12 translation errors that were once tolerated under Sical.

J2450 Translation Quality Metric

Developed in 2000 by the U.S. Engineering Society for Advanced Mobility in Land, Sea, Air and Space, this model is designed to give a "standardized grade" to translations for technical maintenance and repair institutions. The authors of the J2450 guidelines make it very clear that because the focus is technical material, errors of style will not be assessed. The Metric is to be viewed as complementary to the translation service acquisition and management standard being designed by the American Society for Testing and Materials (ASTM).

The evaluator is required to identify and characterize errors according to seven types (wrong term, syntax, omission, word structure/agreement, spelling, punctuation, and other), determine and indicate whether the error is "major" or "minor," and, as in the case of the CTIC model, assign a numerical weight to each error on the basis of characterization (a high of 5, for wrong term, and a low of 2, for punctuation) and seriousness (2 for "major" and 1 for "minor"). The final step is to calculate the total value of the numerical weights and then obtain the "standardized grade" by dividing that total value by the number of words in the source text or sample.

However, the guidelines offer no minimum fixed standard or passing grade or mark; it is the client's responsibility to set such a cutoff point and thus determine the acceptable standard. A corollary of this is that no one type of error renders the translation unacceptable. Indeed, the authors are circumspect on what makes an error major or minor; it inevitably depends, they say, on the evaluator's personal judgment. They do, however, propose a rule of thumb for distinguishing between the two categories: If an error clearly leads to serious *consequences* for a technician or affects the meaning of the translation, it must be considered major. Otherwise, it must be considered minor (Engineering Society for Advanced Mobility 2000: 1).

Another important point to note is that because of the safety considerations inherent in technical documents, the evaluator is directed to select the error type with the higher weight and to opt for "major" over "minor" when in doubt concerning the type and seriousness of an error. Under Sical procedures, the reverse was recommended.

Discourse analysis model
Using works by Searle (1969), Halliday and Hasan (1976), Widdowson (1978), and van Dijk (1980) for the theoretical underpinnings of their model, Bensoussan and Rosenhouse (1990) propose a TQA scheme for *evaluating student translations by discourse analysis.* They make a distinction between errors based on lack of comprehension and those resulting from other shortcomings or problems. Comprehension is assumed to happen simultaneously on the macro and micro levels. Accordingly, they divide errors into (1) macro-level misinterpretations (**frame**, **schema**) and (2) micro-level mistranslations at the utterance (propositional content, communicative function) and word (vocabulary/ expressions, parts of speech/verb tense, pronoun agreement, **acceptability,** and register) levels (1990: 71).

To demonstrate the model, the authors subdivide a chosen (literary) text of approximately 300 words into units ranging from one to three sentences in length, assign it to a group of students as a translation exercise, and proceed to identify and characterize errors at the macro and micro levels, giving points for correct translations of each unit. They then generate frequency tables for each category of error.

They conclude, among other things, that mistranslations at the word level do not automatically lead to misinterpretations of the frame or schema. In other words, the overall message may be preserved in translation, notwithstanding **microtext** error. On this basis they suggest that it may be possible to avoid the cumbersomeness of painstaking micro-evaluation of translations by basing evaluations on misinterpretations alone (Bensoussan and Rosenhouse 1990: 80).

Teleological model
One of the few Canadian theorists to focus on TQA, Larose (1987) makes explicit a quality factor that is only implicit in Sical and SEPT: the objective of the translator. Aware of the dangers of subjectivity and hypercriticism in TQA, Larose issues a salutary warning to the evaluator: "Every translation must be assessed in terms of the appropriateness of the translator's intention to that of the author of the original, not of the appropriateness of the translator's intention to that of the evaluator" (1987: 223; our translation). In making this statement, he is contending that TQA cannot be a closed system, as it has tended

to be in literary-translation criticism; it must take as its starting point the client's and other requirements and goals that the translator has endeavoured to meet.

Larose goes on to propose a multilevel grid for textological TQA, covering microstructures, **macrostructures** (**thematic strings**, **cohesion**, etc.—in short, the overall semantic structure), **superstructure** (narrative and argumentative structures) and external factors, including the conditions of production, intentions, sociocultural background, and so on. Furthermore, the higher the level of the translation error (microstructure being the lowest), the more serious it will be.

In later articles (1994 and 1998), Larose elaborates on the idea of a "**teleological**," criterion-referenced TQA model, contending that TQA can be objective and reliable if the real objectives not of the author but of the translation contract issued by the client are taken into account. Once the objectives are established, the evaluator is in a position to determine the criteria (referential meaning, concision, etc.) and constraints (time, cost, the client's implicit and explicit **quality requirements**, even social values and requirements) against which one or more translations of a source text are to be assessed. The approach is a very pragmatic one: Assessment basically involves comparing the goals of the translator with the resulting translation, in light of pertinent criteria and constraints (1994: 369).

Larose proposes a new grid for a multicriteria analysis in which translations are evaluated against each quality criterion separately and the value of each criterion is weighted according to its importance for the contract. He illustrates the grid with translations of literature, each rendering of lines from Aristophanes's *Lysistrata* being rated against seven criteria: referential meaning, poetic character, humorous imitation of Spartan speech, expression of contrast between Athenian and Spartan speech, rimes, and concision. The criteria may be far removed from those of instrumental translation, but Larose contends that it would certainly be possible to devise a relevant set of criteria for instrumental TQA. He points out that the number of criteria must be limited (fewer than Gouadec's 675!) if the model is to be workable.

Referring to the fact that the Translation Bureau has distanced itself from Sical, Larose notes that there is a fundamental contradiction between sampling for TQA purposes and the contemporary focus on total quality and zero defects. At the same time, he points out that the objective of zero defects is probably unrealistic—hence the Bureau's return to systematic revision of the whole translation (1998: 181).

Larose concedes that the creation of a truly comprehensive TQA grid is probably impossible, because of the number of parameters or criteria, the complexity of their relationships, and the time and resources required to implement it (1998: 175). Accordingly, any grid is necessarily reductionist and based on the most relevant parameters and criteria.

1.1.2. *Non-quantitative models*

Critique productive

Unlike the error-based models above, Antoine Berman's model (1995) incorporates a positive assessment of (literary) translation. Rejecting what he sees as an ideology-driven, judgmental model of TQA, in which the evaluator is intent only on highlighting defects in the target text (TT) or in demonstrating how **norms** in the target culture condition it, Berman advocates an assessment that brings out not only the shortcomings but also the qualities and originality of the translation as a work of art. He then proposes a general procedure. The key step is the selection of significant passages in the translation that encapsulate its essence and comparison of these "zones signifiantes" (1995: 70) with the original. The ensuing "confrontation" may well bring out differences between the source text (ST) and the TT, but they may be assessed as strong points contributing to the originality of the translation.

Berman's is a closed system, and his approach is an empirical one with no specific assessment criteria. His overarching purpose is to demonstrate the superiority of a translation approach that brings out the essence of the original.

Functionalist model

In an attempt to counter what she sees as arbitrary, subjective criticism of literary translations, Katharina Reiss (1971; 2000), an early and leading exponent of the functionalist theory of translation, proposes a method of translation criticism based on text type and goals. After isolating two main translation methods—text-oriented and goal-oriented—Reiss goes on to contend that the critic must assess quality against the standards or criteria appropriate to the method applied. This involves consideration of the linguistic elements of, and extra-linguistic elements affecting, a given text type and the "special function or readership which the translation is intended to serve" (2000: 114). Thus, well before Larose, Reiss brings out the prime importance of the textological and teleological (goals, end use of translation) aspects of TQA. At the same time, she underscores the influence on TQA of the subjective conditions of the hermeneutical process and the translation critic's personality.

Skopostheorie

Christiane Nord (1991a, 1991b, 1992) elaborates on Reiss's (1981) premise of translation as intentional, interlingual communicative action and proposes an analytical model based on the function and intention of the target text in the target culture and applicable to instrumental as much as to literary documents. Depending on the function of the target text and the translation instructions issued by the initiator of the translation request, the translator may intend to preserve all semantic and formal features of the original or adapt the ST material extensively. Thus, she envisages the possibility of establishing **grades** of required types of translation on a scale running from extreme fidelity to extreme liberty (1991b: 28).

Nord's notion of "grades" of translation quality is not comparable to those of Sical or SEPT. Her grades are based on a conscious decision to produce a relatively "literal" or relatively "free" translation and do not encompass a tolerance level for errors unwittingly committed by the translator. It is the "initiator" of the translation project who issues the translation instructions and defines the *skopos*, or prospective target situation (1991b: 8). Accordingly, the evaluator must take the TT *skopos* as the starting point for TQA. Thus Nord's approach closely parallels that of Larose, who emphasizes the need for TQA to factor in reader expectations and the requirements set by the client in the contract.

Nord emphasizes that error analysis is insufficient: "[I]t is the text as a whole whose function(s) and effect(s) must be regarded as the crucial criteria for translation criticism" (1991b: 166). This is a key qualification, for on the basis of a selection of relevant ST features, the translator may eliminate ST items, rely more heavily on implicatures, or "compensate" for them in a different part of the text. Indeed, as van Leuven-Zwart points out in developing an interesting corollary of translation-oriented analysis, the "shifts in meaning" that account for many "unsatisfactory" ratings in professional translation should perhaps not be considered as errors at all, given that equivalence is not feasible (1990: 228–29). In short, microtextual error analysis is insufficient.

In the examples of translation-oriented text analysis presented to illustrate the model, Nord's judgments are generally parameter-specific, and when there is a judgment, it is not definitive. Indeed, she states that there "will be no overall evaluation of the translated texts" (1991b: 226). She does, however, make a definitive, overall judgment on the sample texts as a whole: "[N]one of [the translations] meet the requirements set by text function and recipient orientation" (1991b: 231). But how does she generate an overall assessment from the parameter-specific comparisons, particularly when her judgment is based on the nature of the errors, not their number?

Descriptive-explanatory model

In an update of a work first published in 1977, House (1997) presents a detailed non-quantitative, *descriptive-explanatory* approach to TQA. Like Bensoussan and Rosenhouse, House uses the functional text features explored by Halliday (1978) and Crystal and Davy (1969). She does, however, take issue with the functional approach proposed under **Skopostheorie** because, in her view, it relativizes the importance of the meaning of the source text in favour of the primacy of target-culture norms and purpose. She rejects the principle enunciated by Reiss and Vermeer (1984: 96) that "[t]he purpose of translation determines the means" (our translation). Indeed, she prefaces her presentation of the model with a clear statement of her belief in autonomous meaning of the text and, consequently, the importance of equivalence, although her notion of equivalence is tempered by communicative and pragmatic considerations.

Like Larose and Nord, House calls for a textological approach to TQA: "The importance of the textual aspect of meaning has often been neglected in evaluations of translations, although the necessity of achieving connectivity between successive sentences in another language while at the same time retaining the semantic meaning conveyed in the original is important, especially in covert translation" (1997: 31). Armed with her notion of equivalence based on a distinction between overt (source-text-oriented) and covert (target-text-based) translation, and applying a grid developed from established linguistic theory, House dismisses the idea that TQA is by nature too subjective. At the same time, she does not underestimate the "immense difficulties of empirically establishing what any 'norm of usage' is," especially for the unique situation of an individual text (1997: 18), and of meeting the requirement of knowledge about differences in sociocultural norms (1997: 74). She also concedes that "the relative weighting of individual errors ... is a problem which varies from individual text to individual text" (1997: 45).

House demonstrates the model, identifying and commenting on overt and covert mismatches in a number of sample texts. However, like Nord, she stops short of making a judgment on the translation as a whole, stating that "[i]t is difficult to pass a 'final judgment' on the quality of a translation that fulfils the demands of objectivity" (1997: 119). She ultimately sees her model as descriptive-explanatory, as opposed to a socio-psychologically based value judgment (1997: 116). In other words, TQA should not yield a judgment as to whether the translation meets a specific quality standard, even though House castigates the functionalists for their supposed relativism.

1.2. Investigations and definitions of translation norms

As shown above, all TQA models are concerned with error typology, and the typology differs according to the approach and the linguistic or philosophical theory adopted. In turn, the notion of error is of necessity predicated on a prior notion of acceptability. A number of translation studies experts, all taking an essentially functionalist approach, have focused their attention on defining adequacy or acceptability and, in so doing, have examined what a translation "norm"—on which decisions about acceptability would be based—is and what its sources are, often by drawing on social and philosophical theories of norms.

In keeping with his descriptive-explanatory approach, Toury is critical of translation theorists who endeavour to establish norms, rules, or directives on how to translate because their pronouncements are, in his view, based on insufficient empirical data. Normative statements are all prescriptive ("should," "must"), but in actual translation practice may be little more than recommendations: "... there is absolutely no certainty that a normative pronouncement would draw on, or even reflect, any kind of behaviour which is truly regular within the culture it purports to represent. Moreover, in spite of the authoritative tone in which it is often presented, ignoring it would not necessarily call for any sanctions. In other words, directives that do not reflect any existing behaviour would not unconditionally create new behavioural patterns either" (1994: 261–62).

Toury prefers to define norms as "explanatory hypotheses" emerging from regularities in translation behaviour rather than entities in their own right (1999: 16). He also maintains that translation-specific norms (e.g., how to translate metaphors) are distinct from other communication (**target language**) norms and, in particular, those of translation assessment: "[T]ranslations are the result of a direct application of **translation norms**, whereas assessments employ first and foremost norms of evaluation and evaluation-presentation, including the norms governing the composition of evaluative texts. As regards translational norms, evaluators just react to them and their results" (1999: 23). Evaluators and translators may favour different blends of **adequacy** (fidelity to ST) and acceptability (fidelity to TT). In short, TQA and, indeed, any attempt to define or impart the way "good" translations are to be done are fraught with difficulty.

Toury will go no further in establishing translation norms or standards. Norms are exerted by the target language and culture in terms of expectations of what a translation should be and what its relationship to the source text should be—that is, where on the adequacy (fidelity to ST)–acceptability (fidelity to TT) continuum it should be positioned (1981: 24).

Several other theorists have elaborated on Toury's line of thought, including Christiane Nord (1991a). She makes a distinction between translation rules, norms, and **conventions**. To illustrate the differences, she cites *grammar* rules (imposed by an authority and coupled with penalties), *stylistic* norms (specific performance instructions not associated with penalties), and *text type* or *speech act* conventions (neither explicitly stated nor binding, and based on common knowledge and expectation) (1991a: 97).

She goes on to discuss translation norms and rules within a broader framework of translation conventions by analogy with Searle's regulative and constitutive rules (Searle 1969: 33–42):

> Regulative translational conventions refer to the generally accepted forms of handling certain translation problems below the text rank (e.g., proper names, culture-bound realities or realia, quotations, etc.), whereas constitutive conventions determine what a particular culture community accepts as a translation (as opposed to an adaptation or version or other forms of intercultural text transfer). The sum total of constitutive conventions forms the general concept of translation prevailing in a particular culture community. (Nord 1991a: 100)

This conventional concept reflects the "standards" (not defined by Nord) that both users and translators expect a translation to meet in terms of its relationship with the source text.

Thus, like Toury, Nord sees normative statements, be they rules, norms, or regulative conventions, as generally bearing on discrete elements of the interlingual communication process, as directions on how a specific type of ST feature should be rendered in the TT. Using Skopostheorie as her reference point and recognizing that such normative statements are often vague, they may contradict one another, and, as such, they pose a serious problem for trainees, she proposes a broader "norm of functionality" to which all translations must adhere. The translator must follow the translation instructions—the explicit, detailed requirements regarding the scope and function of the proposed translation—in order to comply with the norm of functionality. The translation will then "achieve the function or functions required by the target situation, and its form [will] conform to the target culture conventions valid for the text type in question" (1991a: 107). Nord is thus proposing a new norm as a broader, "stringent frame of reference" for translation choices.

Chesterman (1997), who, like Toury and Nord, puts the issue of translation norms in a sociocultural context, splits translation-related norms into *professional* (process) norms and *expectancy* (product) norms. Professional norms, based on the behaviour of the best translators, are of three types: *accountability* (akin to Nord's principle of loyalty to all parties concerned); *communication* (the optimization of communication in its widest sense); and *relation* (maintaining an appropriate relation between ST and TT—akin to Toury's notion of adequacy).

Expectancy norms pertain to the expectations of the target readership regarding the quality of the target language—its grammaticalness (rules of grammar) and acceptability/appropriateness (norms of usage). These norms may be qualitative (specific stylistic or usage requirements, established by norm authorities such as reputable style guides) or quantitative (generally accepted sentence length or proportion of relative clauses in a scientific text, for example).

Like Toury, Chesterman sees norms as emerging from the notion of "regularity." If a given strategy is used regularly not by translators in general but by *competent professional translators* who are aiming for compliance with professional and expectancy norms, "it will *de facto* take on the status of ... a *normative law*" (1993: 14). Because they are recognized as being maximally compatible with professional and expectancy norms, they have prescriptive force. Thus Chesterman establishes his own hierarchy: translation laws and strategies, normative laws (norm-directed strategies observed to be used by a large proportion of competent translators), and norms.

Toury's, Nord's, and Chesterman's approaches to norms share two important characteristics: (1) they are prospective (a priori), rather than retrospective (a posteriori), and are intended more as guidelines for translators than as elements of a TQA framework; (2) with the exception of the very broad norms of adequacy, acceptability, and functionality, they establish requirements pertaining to specific aspects of translation and target-language usage, not quality standards against which a translation can be assessed or graded.

Unlike the theorists, translation practitioners have taken an interest in official, broad "standards" in order to ensure that the translation industry is part of the "total quality" and "continuous improvement" trend that has gained considerable currency both in government and in the private sector (see *Circuit* 1994; *Language International* 1998). The focus has been on ensuring that translation production procedures are consistent with those required under ISO 9000 standards.

Austria, Italy, and Germany have gone as far as to issue their own national translation standards, and a working group is developing a European standard (Société française des traducteurs 2003). Note, however, that what is to be standardized is not the level of quality of a translation but a set of procedures for achieving that level. Sturz explains the limits of the German standard (DIN 2345):

> The important issue of measuring the quality of translations by rating them ... cannot be solved by a standard. However, a standard can provide specific rules for the evaluation process. Such measures ... include completeness, terminological correctness, grammar and style, as well as adherence to a style guide agreed to between the buyer and the translator. ... DIN 2345 is not a certification standard. (Sturz, 1998: 19, 41)

In fact, what the translation standard offers is a set of "normative statements" about the various parameters of translation, and as such it echoes the concepts developed by the functional translation theorists referred to above.

1.3. Present state: conclusions and issues

1.3.1. TQA models

We can draw a number of conclusions from our overview:

(1) Quantitative models are for the most part microtextual, with assessment generally operating at the subsentence

level (Translation Bureau, CTIC, GTS, J2450), even where sampling and the selection of short passages for error analysis appear to have been discarded.

(2) The relative seriousness (weighting) of errors is based on a binary (minor/major) structure (Sical, GTS) or a more complex points system (CTIC, SEPT, J2450).

(3) A number of criterion-referenced models (Bensoussan and Rosenhouse, Larose, Nord, House) are based not only on the microtextual features of the text but also on discursive features such as **coherence** and cohesion. However, they have not been developed with a broad range of instrumental translation types and subject fields in mind and are demonstrated with reference only to short texts.

(4) The demise of Sical III also signalled the demise of the standards-referenced model, unless we consider "zero defects" as a standard. The quantitative, microtextual models have, in one sense, moved closer to the textological models and become criterion-referenced, factoring in the specific conditions and objectives surrounding production of the translation. The evaluator's "judgment" effectively becomes a catch-all solution to many TQA problems, and there is no transparent means of "settling" borderline cases.

(5) The theoretical basis for the textological models that are actually demonstrated is taken primarily from Halliday, Crystal and Davy, van Dijk, Widdowson, and Searle. Argumentation theory has not been tested as a potential TQA tool.

(6) None of the textological models proposes clearly defined *overall* quality or tolerance levels. House refuses to pass overall judgments, and Nord's assessments are not related to a scale of measurable values. As McAleester remarks, "[I]n no case is any suggestion made concerning the amount and gravity of errors that can be tolerated for the total translation to be considered adequate" (2000: 234). Further, as Chesterman points out, the models provide for assessment against specific parameters or functions, not against all parameters or functions combined. This inevitably militates against global assessment unless translations are found wanting in all departments.

(7) Gouadec, Bensoussan and Rosenhouse, Larose, and Nord all recognize and emphasize the interrelationship between the

translation unit and the **macrotext** in terms of the impact and seriousness of error. However, no definition of error gravity has been proposed on a scientific, theoretical, textological basis, and evaluators have to rely on ill-defined concepts such as "complete failure to render the meaning" and "essential part of the message." How is the "essential part" to be determined, and can "partial" failure not be just as damaging to an essential part of the message?

(8) As a corollary of (7), the theorists shy away from standards as such, preferring to propose or identify *norms*, *rules*, and *conventions* pertaining to discrete translation elements and parameters. Likewise, recently issued national standards are not tools for assessing quality but guidelines for ensuring that quality is achieved.

1.4. Objectives

It is in response to the above conclusions and issues that I will propose an argumentation-centred approach to assessment and develop, for the purpose of determining the quality of professional translations for delivery to clients, a TQA model that is text-based but also flexible enough to incorporate microtextual TQA for specific purposes such as target-language quality assessment. In the process, I will establish a minimum level of acceptable overall quality for instrumental translations, thus avoiding the problem of how to graduate from assessment against discrete criteria to a measurement of overall quality, and I will propose a means of measuring quality of texts of varying lengths while avoiding the pitfalls of sampling and quantification.

I also propose a new definition of translation error providing a coherent, defensible concept for error analysis and assessment. The definition of major/critical error, around which the determination of minimum acceptable quality revolves, will be based not only on empirical judgment but also on established theory, and will confirm Larose's statement that the higher in the macrostructure the error occurs, the more serious it is.

Finally, I respond to the lack of a specific, fixed translation quality standard by proposing a draft standard that incorporates actual quality levels in a textological framework.

CHAPTER TWO

OVERVIEW OF ARGUMENTATION FRAMEWORK AND ARGUMENT SCHEMA

> ... la fonction rhétorique est elle-même transcendante par rapport aux autres fonctions du langage. L'intention rhétorique perturbe virtuellement le fonctionnement des différents aspects du procès linguistique.
>
> (J. Dubois et al. 1970)

The value of argumentation theory as the basis for a TQA model resides in the fact that it brings out the interrelationship and interdependence of the individual **propositions**, on the one hand, and the reasoning process and development of arguments and messages flowing through the text, on the other. Argumentation and the means of persuasion, or rhetoric, are not the preserve of political, legal, and religious **discourse** alone. Research over the last few decades has shown that rhetoric is an important feature of writing in a broad range of fields, including psychology (Billig 1996), law (Perelman and Olbrechts-Tyteca, 1969, Perelman, 1977; Rybacki 1996), history (Greimas 1983), economics (McCloskey 1985), logic (Thomas 1986; Walton 1989), education (Andrews 1996), the environment (Myerson and Rydin 1996), and the natural sciences (Ouellet 1984, 1985, 1992; McGuire and Melia 1989, 1991; Gross 1991). It has been demonstrated that even in writing in the natural sciences and economics, in which observation, objectivity, and accurate measurement supposedly obviate the need for rhetoric, the tools of argumentation are omnipresent. One of the main reasons for the presence of rhetoric in science, it is suggested, is that information, knowledge, and ideas are just as argumentative, and arguable, as beliefs and hopes, particularly in today's society of information overload.

Note, too, that the modern proponents of argumentation theory do not present rhetoric in a negative light. Whereas the study of rhetoric had since the Middle Ages been restricted to aesthetics and the analysis of figures of speech, the "New Rhetoric" has rehabilitated the argumentation aspect of rhetoric as an integral part of the creation and communication of knowledge:

> Why should the latest facts not be persuasive? They will not speak for themselves. Why should theories not be articulated? They will not be heard otherwise. Rhetoric, the approach, looks at rhetoric, the language. It asks what the words are doing ... why these words are chosen to convey the facts and theories. ... Rhetoric is about academic discourse and newspapers, specialist articles and policies, working papers and headlines. The texts are different, and some are scientific; but science also argues and persuades. (Myerson and Rydin 1996: 16)

So even discourse that is strictly informational is arguable; once there is content to convey, an **argument** is present, and it transcends and affects all other aspects of the discourse.

2.1. Logic, argument, and rhetoric

Before going further, we should define our terms. Logic involves scientific inquiry into the very structure of argument and its validity: valid premises yielding a valid conclusion make for a coherent, consistent argument at an abstract level. Formal and informal logic are typified by the exploitation of deductive reasoning and the syllogism.

Modern proponents of argumentation theory define argument as reasoned discourse (Billig 1996: 74) that draws on logic, among other means, in order to be effective. At the same time, argument is an instance of social interaction and, as such, extends beyond the abstractions of logic to human affairs and the exploitation of non-scientific language. Billig and others build on Bakhtin's theories to show that reasoned discourse is essentially **dialogical**: every argument (logos) elicits a counterargument (antilogos), and every statement presupposes a question. This dynamic applies not only to spoken dialogue (conversation) but also to written discourse.

The fact that argument is dialogical and functions in real-world situations carries other implications. First, once argument goes beyond deductive logic and penetrates the realm of human affairs, whether it be law, economics, literature, ethics, or business, conclusions are no longer absolutely correct but *probable*, because truth cannot be ascertained as readily as in science and logic (Corbett and Connors, 1999: 53). Second, each conclusion or argument can be disconfirmed: it is "defeasible." Antaki (1994: 144–45) cites inductive reasoning as the best-known type of defeasible argument in that it can be disconfirmed by new facts.

Argument, as reasoned discourse, is a component of rhetoric, defined by Corbett and Connors (1999: 1) as "the art of the discipline that deals with the use of discourse, either spoken or written, to inform or persuade or motivate an audience, whether that audience is made up of one person or a group of persons." As the art of persuasion, rhetoric (in its classical form) comprises five functions, including the discovery (*inventio*) of arguments, the arrangement (*dispositio*) of the parts of the discourse, and style (*elocutio*). It is with the help of these last two components that arguments achieve their purpose.

Assigning these broad definitions to argument and rhetoric, Billig, Antaki, and others contend that all texts are, to varying degrees, argumentative. Andrews reiterates Habermas's point that "any utterance necessarily carries with it a suite of claims which, if accepted, give the utterance legitimacy, and that even what seem to be bald reports will necessarily carry a weight of ... claims" (Andrews 1995: 170). Thomas, for his part, prefers to talk of "reasoned discourses," while allowing "arguments" as a synonym: "These discourses consist of one or more sentences containing some sentences that are set forth as making probable, proving, justifying or explaining other statements in the same discourse" (1986: 10). Thus all forms of instrumental discourse—not only argument but also narrative, description, explanation, and dialogue—are to some extent grounded in argument because they are instances of reasoned discourse, although the invention of argument will be more prominent in the expository (explanatory) and argumentative modes (Corbett and Connors 1999: 85).

2.2. Features of an argumentation-centred TQA model

My overall model draws on two groups of sources: first, philosopher Stephen Toulmin's analysis of argument structure and the work of some other philosophers and linguists who have focussed on issues of reasoning, coherence, and cohesion in discourse; second, the New Rhetoric of Perelman and others, which is a modern application of Aristotle's analysis and categorization of argumentation and of the underlying values.

Expanding the three components of rhetoric referred to above (invention of arguments, arrangement/order of arguments, and style), I propose to develop my model on the basis of the following discourse categories:

1. Argument schema

2. Rhetorical topology
   (a) Organizational relations
   (b) Connectives (conjunctives and other inference indicators)
   (c) Propositional functions
   (d) Types of argument
   (e) Figures
   (f) Narrative strategy

2.3. Argument schema

Toulmin and his colleagues explore arguments in a variety of areas of specialization and draw the conclusion that the components of an argument are essentially the same in all fields and types of text. They go on to propose a set of elements that are required for an argument in any field—**claims/discoveries**, **grounds**, **warrants/rules**, and **backings**—and two elements that may be required—**qualifiers/modalizers** and **rebuttals/exceptions/restrictions** (Toulmin et al., 1984: 25). A brief explanation and illustration of each of these terms follows.

2.3.1. *Claim/discovery (C)*

The claim (or discovery) is the conclusion of the argument, or the main point toward which all the other elements of the argument converge. The following claims are typical of instrumental texts for translation:

- recommendations in a policy document or discussion paper
- a request for a specific amount in a grant application to a government agency
- the announcement of a new health program
- a claim of high energy efficiency of natural gas-heated homes in a survey report
- the judge's decision in an appeal case

- the classification of a newly discovered plant as belonging to a particular order

The areas of specialization are varied, and so are the purposes of discourse—to make a recommendation, a request, a public announcement, a claim of superior performance, a legal decision, or an announcement of a scientific discovery.

2.3.2. *Grounds (G)*

Claims are not freestanding; they have to be supported by one or more pieces of information, which form the grounds of the argument. These are facts, oral testimony, matters of common knowledge, well-known truisms or commonsense observations, historical reports, and so on, upon which the sender and recipient of the message can agree.

The grounds for announcement of a new health program may be the observation, or report, of overcrowding in emergency departments of hospitals. Note that a claim may be based on more than one ground. For example, the announcement may also be prompted by an infusion of new funds into the national or provincial health budget.

2.3.3. *Warrant (W)*

Warrants are statements indicating how the facts, observations, and other elements in the grounds are connected to the claim or conclusion. In our health program example, the logical connection between overcrowding in emergency departments and the new health program is the requirement for rapid response implicit in the emergency department's mandate. However, warrants are not self-validating; they must draw their strength from other considerations, known as backing.

2.3.4. *Backing (B)*

The backing is the overarching principle, value, law, or standard governing the issue at hand. In the health program example, the principle of universality enshrined in the *Canada Health Act,* along with human and social values of caring for the sick, would provide support for all the other elements adduced to justify introduction of the new program.

Note that the warrant and the backing may be implicit; they may be presuppositions underlying the communication situation. It is this fact that makes the argument schema different from the overt *dispositio* of the argument.

2.3.5. *Qualifier (Q)/modalizer*

The qualifier or modalizer is a statement or phrase that enhances or mitigates the force of the claim. Thus the new health program may "definitely," "certainly," "probably" or "possibly" be introduced.

Toulmin and his colleagues stress the importance of qualifying (or modalizing) statements in the argument structure: "Their function is to indicate the kind of *rational strength* to be attributed to C [claim] on the basis of its relationship to G [grounds], W [warrant], and B [backing]" (Toulmin et al., 1984: 86). Accordingly, the translation evaluator should pay particular attention to the treatment of qualifiers in the target text, and for the purposes of this study we will have to consider how much weight to place on failure to render qualifiers in the TT.

2.3.6. *Rebuttal/exception/restriction (R)*

This takes the form of a statement of extraordinary or exceptional circumstances that contradicts or may undermine the force of the supporting arguments. It is often introduced for the sake of caution or modesty. Thus, in our example, the new health program will be introduced "unless the government's fiscal situation worsens."

2.3.7. *Example*

Depending on the complexity of the argument, the claim may be based on several grounds, each of which would require its own B-W-G-C structure. In such an instance, the ground itself becomes a claim that needs to be supported. Furthermore, a long document may contain a number of claims of equal importance, all of which would require support in the interest of sound argument. As a result, the argument structure of the full text will reflect a chain of arguments.

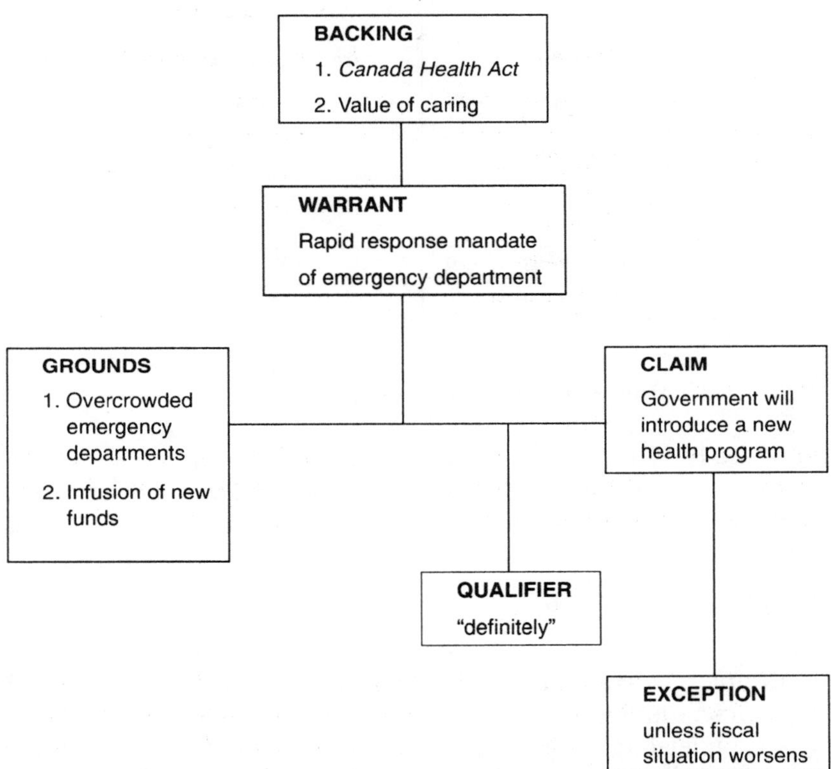

2.3.8. *Generic framework*

Therefore, assuming Toulmin's premise that texts in all fields present essentially the same argumentative structure, we already have a generic working framework for our TQA model inasmuch as one of the evaluator's tasks will be to *determine whether the basic argument elements (B, W, G, C, Q, R) are accurately rendered in the TT if they are present in the ST*. The provisional base grid could take the form below:

Element	Translation assessment
Claim/discovery	
Grounds	
Warrant	
Backing	
Qualifier/modalizer	
Rebuttal/Restriction	

2.3.9. *Preliminary application of model*

Let us see how the schema can be applied in translation. The source text below is a passage from a document presenting recommendations regarding potential sources of statistical data for an energy efficiency study.

> SOURCE TEXT
>
> Rappelons également le [travail de modélisation fait par le Compendium lors du projet sur les séries de données nationales à compléter, qui a été réalisé dans le cadre du plan de travail de l'an passé (voir Boucher et Bonin, mai 2000). Ce projet a permis de combler le vide entre l'ECC at l'ENUVeP et d'obtenir, entre autres, des séries complètes sur la distance annuelle parcourue en moyenne par une voiture de 1980 à 1996 et par un camion léger de 1982 à 1996].
>
> [...]
>
> **L'intérêt du précédent projet est qu'il fournit des estimations de la distance parcourue qui fluctuent au fil des années au lieu de considérer les valeurs constantes, comme cela semble être le cas présentement dans le modèle.** <u>Par contre, les données ne sont pas disponibles en fonction de l'âge exact des véhicules, mais plutôt suivant quatre groupes d'âge : 2 ans et moins, 3-5 ans, 6-8 ans, 9 ans et plus</u>. *La possibilité de produire, à l'aide des outils d'analyse bayesienne développés par Mme Nathalie Boucher, des séries équivalentes à l'échelle*

provinciale ou régionale (Maritimes, Québec, Ontario, Prairies, Colombie-Britannique) devrait être étudiée lors d'une prochaine entente.

TARGET TEXT

We also recall that [modelling work was done by the Compendium for the project on the national data series to complete what was done for the work plan last year (see Boucher and Bonin, May 2000). This project made it possible to fill the gap between FCS and NaPVUS and obtain, among others, complete series of annual distance travelled on average by a car from 1980 to 1996 and by a light truck from 1982 to 1996].

[...]

The advantage of the previous project is that it provides estimates for the distance travelled that fluctuate with the years instead of being considered constant values, as it seems to be the case currently with this model. However, the data is not available according to the exact age of the vehicles, but rather according to age groups: 2 years and under, 3-5 years, 6-8 years, 9 years and over. *The possibility, by using Bayesian analysis tools developed by Ms Nathalie Boucher, of producing series equivalent to the provincial or regional scale (Maritimes, Quebec, Ontario, Prairies, British Columbia) should be studied for the next agreement.*

Analysis
The first step is to establish the argument schema. Thus,

claim	= recommendation that potential for generating data series at provincial/regional level by means of specific tools be examined (italics)
grounds	= value of earlier project and specific tools used for it (boldface)
warrant	= 1. authority, reliability, and achievements of research organization (Compendium); 2. management rigour (work plan) (square brackets)
backing	= scientism (presupposed)
qualifier	= force of modal verb in claim (double underlining)
restriction	= limitation on data available (underlining)

The presupposed backing is the objectivity and accuracy of, and accordingly the confidence placed in, the scientific approach in statistics. The backing reinforces the warrant, comprising the specific authority, work and approach of the research organization concerned. This in turn supports the grounds—the value of the earlier project—for the claim (recommendation), which is expressed by a forceful qualifier in the form of a modal verb. The author places a restriction on the claim, however, by indicating that the data available from the earlier project may not be as precise as required.

The second step is to establish, through comparative reading, to what extent the argument schema is reflected in the TT. We find that the translator has misconstrued both the warrant ("to complete what was done for" instead of "to be completed as part of") and the claim ("producing series equivalent to" instead of "producing equivalent provincial or regional series"). We then complete the preliminary TQA grid as follows:

Element	**Translation assessment**
Claim/discovery	Inaccurately rendered
Grounds	Accurately rendered
Warrant	Inaccurately rendered
Backing	N/A (not present in ST)
Qualifier	Accurately rendered
Rebuttal/restriction	Accurately rendered

At this stage we have been able to identify the argument schema, or what Walton (1989: 114) calls the "semantic core," of ST and TT, and to establish the degree of correspondence between them. We have not yet developed a means of determining the impact of non-correspondence of one or more elements on an overall assessment of the schema in translation, nor have we considered what kind of assessment, if any, should be made at the microtextual level.

Following up on Bensoussan and Rosenhouse's suggestion that assessment of text-level misinterpretations may avoid the cumbersomeness of other TQA tools (see 1.1.1), I have established a limited set of six elements on which assessment of overall quality of a professional translation is to be based.

CHAPTER THREE

RHETORICAL TOPOLOGY

3.1. Elements of the topology

The evaluator would expect the professional to identify, understand, and accurately render the macroelements of a text's argumentation (reasoning) structure. If the translator meets these requirements, he or she will have gone a long way toward conveying to the TT readership the central message(s) of the text. However, the translator will not meet the requirements fully unless he or she understands and accurately renders not only the macroelements but also the network that they form—that is, their interrelationships, and how the writer of the source text brings out those interrelationships and reinforces the argument accordingly.

Graphically, the macroelements are nodes joined by lines (see diagram, 2.3.7). But what do those lines represent? In fact, they are the arguments themselves, the chain of statements that justify the claims.

Therefore, the next step in refining our TQA model is to explore the various types of argument in instrumental texts, their foundations, their structures, and their interconnections. In so doing, we will be examining the linkages between the schema and textual elements at a more microtextual, but not necessarily sentence or subsentence, level. From a TQA perspective, our task will be to determine whether the specific processes of getting from grounds to claim in the ST are accurately rendered in the TT, including the role of individual arguments and rhetorical devices and their treatment in the TT.

What we will be examining are, to use Vignaux's terminology, "argumentative operations" and "logical operations." For Vignaux, the progression of a text depends on the use of local (microtextual) procedures that combine to form a "rhetorical topology" (1976: 97–98). The use of the word "topology" is particularly interesting in that it focuses our attention on the arrangement of arguments and their interrelationships: the argumentative structure of the text is flexible, like the geometrical shape, and can change with the arrangement (*dispositio*) of arguments and development and use of various argumentative, logical, and other operations in the text.

Rhetoric being the art of persuasion, Vignaux points out that the arrangement of arguments is a prime means of affecting the audience or readership. In fact, the topology—the interaction of, and connections between, the propositions making up the text—is the argumentative strategy at play. *Thus, from a TQA perspective, we must determine whether the topology present in the ST and the rhetorical features within the topology, all of which are designed to achieve, or which tend to achieve, a given effect, are parallelled by a TT topology and rhetorical features tending toward the same or a similar effect.* In so doing, we will examine six key components:

- The binary organization of text content, which is closely related to argument schema (Mendenhall 1990).
- The manifestation—primarily in the form of conjunctives—of the linkages between propositions that make up arguments and between arguments that make up texts. In this context, Vignaux refers to "logical operators" such as causal, additive, and adversative conjunctions as means of formalizing and signalling to the reader the structure and direction of arguments, and he stresses the importance of the position of these operators in terms of the arrangement of arguments (1976: 55).
- Propositions and the dynamic relations between them. Here we will use Widdowson's (1978) model of propositional functions.
- The types of arguments themselves.
- Figures of speech. Aristotle's particular interests were the metaphor and periodic style as a support to argumentation, as means of "clarifying and of making the speech lively and attractive" (Ryan, 1984: 166), but the work of Angenot, Hamon, Halsall, and others who built on the New Rhetoric model has brought to light many figures that, far from being merely stylistic or "ornamental," enhance, or are integral parts of, arguments in a wide variety of fields.

  Figures usually function at the microtextual, tactical level of discourse, but they can also be macrotextual, as in the case of certain analogies and extended metaphors.
- Narrative strategy. Our analysis will focus on the presence/absence of the implicit author and the devices used to present opinion as fact in the text.

Argumentation thus operates through several mechanisms, and in order to transfer the semantic and pragmatic content of the source text, the translator must grasp both the individual argumentative features and the interrelations of the different mechanisms. Note also that the components of rhetorical topology are by no means restricted to the microtextual level: an organizational relation can represent the content structure of the whole text; a single argument from cause can reflect the argument schema of the text; a single figure (analogy, irony, antithesis) can cover the whole text; and the narrative strategy operates at text level.

3.2. Organizational relations

I have already outlined the *dispositio*, or classical arrangement, of the argumentative text (see 2.1). We can look at the overall structure (superstructure) of the text in another way—as a body of speech acts organized in such a way as to achieve the purpose of the text: to inform, explain, solve a problem, justify a position, evaluate, persuade, and so on. According to Mendenhall (1990: 49), two main organizational frameworks are possible: the conjunctive framework and the hierarchical framework.

In the conjunctive framework, the acts are independent of one another. They nonetheless combine to achieve a purpose. A weather forecast listing the sequence of meteorological events expected in the coming hours or days would reflect such a framework.

The hierarchical framework is more common in instrumental texts. Here, there is a central, independent (nuclear) proposition—corresponding to the purpose of the text or given part of a text—upon which other, dependent (satellite) propositions act on the basis of a specific type of relation. Mendenhall (1990: 50) lists among the main types problem–solution; conclusion–reason; action–motivation; situation–background; action–justification; opinion–evidence; action–means; thesis–antithesis; goal–means; whole–part; process–stage; assertion–proof; and question–answer.

Organizational relations permeate discourse, between sentences, between paragraphs, and between the various parts of a text. As such, they operate at both the microtextual and macrotextual levels. Indeed, at the highest level, they are an integral part of the argument schema in that they represent the specific links between the macrostructural elements.

Thus, in the health care example, the relations between grounds (delays and overcrowding in emergency departments; availability of funds) and claim (new program) are those of problem–solution and goal–means. The explanatory mode typical of scientific and technical discourse may be reflected in the process–stage or thesis–development relation (report on testing a hypothesis, IT user guide, etc.), but it is also typical of the social sciences and may be reflected in the goal–means or problem–solution relation in a policy document. Texts of a more argumentative nature may be based on the thesis–antithesis relation.

For argumentation-centred TQA purposes, we will determine the arrangement, or organizational relations, in the ST and then assess the degree to which the TT reflects that arrangement or pattern.

3.3. Conjunctives and other inference indicators

The progression of ideas in a text is signposted and enhanced by connectors (conjunctives and other inference indicators) that signal logical relations between propositions and guide the reader through the argumentation, performing an essentially interpretive function in relation to the text as a whole (Reboul and Moeschler 1998b: 96). They therefore play a critical role, which needs to be examined in the context of TQA.

Another reason for incorporating conjunctive forms into our study is that they are frequently misinterpreted, even by seasoned translators, with the result that logical connections established in the ST are lost, and even reversed, in the TT. In translation between English and French, the following conjunctives, in particular, are a recurrent source of difficulty:

- *Par ailleurs*—can be adversative (however) or additive (moreover)
- *Or* (French)—can be adversative or additive
- *En effet*—is additive, but if translated by *in fact,* may be misinterpreted as an adversative
- *Ainsi*—can be additive (*for example*) or causal
- *D'autre part*—can be adversative or additive
- *Thus*—can be causal or additive
- *In fact*—can be adversative or additive

Reboul and Moeschler refer to the four types of connector established by Roulet et al. (1985: 112):

- **argumentative**—indicates that the proposition following is an argument for the preceding, central proposition. Examples are *car, en effet, d'ailleurs, au moins, puisque, parce que, comme,* and *même*. To use Thomas's vocabulary, they introduce reasons justifying, proving, explaining, or reinforcing a conclusion or claim.
- **conclusive/consecutive**—indicates that the proposition following relates, as a logical deduction or effect, to a preceding argument for it. Examples are *donc, alors, aussi, ainsi,* and *par conséquent*. They signal a reason–conclusion relation.
- **counter-argumentative**—indicates a counter-argument to the central proposition. Examples are *mais, bien que, quand même, cependant, néanmoins,* and *pourtant*. They signal Mendenhall's thesis–antithesis, thesis–concession, and statement–denial relations.
- **re-evaluative**—indicates that the proposition following implies a review or reassessment of the central proposition. Examples are *finalement, en somme, en fin de compte, de toute façon, au fond, décidément,* and *bref*. This type introduces a conclusion derived not from the immediately preceding statement but from a review of a cluster of preceding statements.

Their categorization is invaluable because it brings out the role of the conjunctive in argumentation. For English, I will base my study in large part on Halliday and Hasan's (1976) breakdown into four types of conjunctive:

- **causal**—*so, therefore, as a result, with this in mind, it follows, in such an event,* and so on. The relationships between the various components of Toulmin's argument schema are mainly causal. The reason invoked for the claim resides in the grounds, the justification for the grounds is the warrant, and so on. Examination of the treatment of causal conjunctives in particular must therefore be an integral part of an argumentation-centred TQA model.

- **adversative**—*yet, however, nevertheless, in fact, on the other hand, at the same time,* and so on. This group, too, is of considerable importance to argumentation, as in discussion documents on the pros and cons of actions and policies and in arguments in which the writer is endeavouring to highlight a dichotomy (argument by dissociation) between two concepts or situations.
- **additive**—*furthermore, moreover, in addition, alternatively, similarly, in other words, for example,* and so on. Additive conjunctives are commonly found in translations of texts in which points are explained, exemplified, and emphasized.
- **temporal**—*then, next, secondly, previously, finally, at last, first ... then, at first ... in the end, in short, to sum up,* and so on. Commonly associated with narrative documents, this type of conjunctive can also play an important role in the ordering of ideas in more clearly argumentative material.

Halliday and Hasan's categories parallel those of Reboul and Moeschler up to a point: their causal conjunctives are equivalent to the consecutive ones above, and their adversative conjunctives are equivalent to the counter-argumentative ones. However, the argumentative connectors above are either additive or causal for Halliday and Hasan, and the re-evaluative ones can be additive, temporal, or adversative. Note also that Roulet et al. include conjunctions linking subordinate and main clauses in their four categories. However, we will be concentrating here on connectors linking sentences and co-ordinate clauses.

According to Halliday and Hasan, the distinctive characteristic of conjunctives (subsuming, for our purposes, what they call conjunctive and discourse adjuncts) is that they are cohesive "by virtue of their specific meaning ... they express certain meanings which presuppose the presence of other components in the discourse" (1976: 226). In other words, the nature of the cohesive relation is semantic, as opposed to the relatedness of form generated by substitution and ellipsis and the relatedness of reference caused by pronouns, demonstratives, and reiteration. Further, those meanings can be external (connections between "events") or internal (connections between elements of the discourse, or argument)—hence the importance of this particular type of connector to our premises. This does not mean, however, that other types of cohesion cannot play a role in argumentation.

3.3.1. *Illustration of treatment of four conjunctive types in instrumental translation*

Causal

Subject: description of the historical development and situation of the co-operative movement in Europe

> ST
>
> De plus, comme l'action du tiers système s'est orientée vers la production de biens et de services, avec des intensités et selon des modalités variables suivant les pays, elle s'est trouvée en relation avec le marché. *D'où* une conceptualisation contemporaine qui insiste sur la dimension intermédiaire des phénomènes désignés sous l'appellation générique de tiers secteur.
>
> TT
>
> In addition, since the third system has focussed, to different degrees and under conditions that vary from country to country, on the production of goods and services, it has established a relationship with the market. *The outcome is* a concept that emphasizes the intermediary dimension of phenomena referred to collectively as the third sector.

The conjunctive is an external causal: the writer has presented the historical development of the third sector in the economy (co-operatives). In the TT, it is replaced with a noun, *outcome*, exemplifying lexical cohesion.

Adversative

Subject: inventory of sources of information for statistical surveys

> ST
>
> Il était convenu dans le cadre de l'entente de 1999-2000 de limiter la révision de l'inventaire aux fiches jugées prioritaires. Étant donné la date de la dernière mise à jour complète, il a *toutefois* été observé que la presque totalité des fiches demandaient à être révisées, ne serait-ce que pour valider les noms et coordonnées des personnes responsables des sources inventoriées.
>
> TT
>
> It was agreed in the 1999–2000 agreement to limit the inventory revision to priority files. Considering the date of the last complete

> update, *we maintained that* almost every file needed to be revised, if only to validate the names and addresses of the persons responsible for the inventoried sources.

Note that the translator fails to provide any equivalent for the external adversative in the ST and, by misinterpreting the finite verb in the second sentence, misconstrues the chronology of reported events: the observation took place during the revision of the inventory. As a result, the adversative logical connection between the two propositions is lost.

Additive
Subject: inventory of sources of information for statistical surveys

> ST
> Il est à noter que la source T-YA02 a été incluse même s'il s'agit d'une source américaine car elle contient plusieurs points qui entrent en relation avec la source T-DP09, fiche déjà rattachée à l'inventaire et également d'origine américaine. *De plus,* les données de ces deux enquêtes américaines constituent un point de référence utile pour les données canadiennes.
>
> *D'autre part,* quelques modifications se sont avérées nécessaires dans la mise en forme du site Web, afin d'améliorer la présentation générale de l'inventaire et de clarifier la définition de certains champs.
>
> TT
> Note that, even though it is American, source T-YA02 was included because it contains many points relating to source T-DP09, another American file already included in the inventory. *Furthermore,* the data in these two American surveys make a useful point of reference for Canadian data.
>
> *Moreover,* to improve the general presentation of the inventory and to clarify the definition of certain fields, some changes to the web site format were proved necessary.

The translator renders the additive force of the conjunctives, although *D'autre part* can be adversative. It is the translator's ability to determine the nature of the connection between the two propositions in this case, not the conjunctive itself, that ensures accurate transfer.

Temporal
Subject: inventory of sources of information for statistical surveys

> ST
> L'inventaire comprenait alors 65 fiches au total. Nous avons fait *en premier lieu* un appel à tous via le bulletin d'information du Compendium de septembre dernier afin de sensibiliser les gens et de les encourager à valider les données des fiches sous leur responsabilité. *Ensuite,* nous sommes entrés en communication avec les personnes contacts (ou les personnes répondantes, selon les situations) soit par téléphone, soit par courrier électronique, soit par télécopieur. Nous leur demandions *alors* de vérifier si toutes les informations inscrites dans les fiches décrivant leurs données étaient encore d'usage aujourd'hui et si certaines informations devaient être ajoutées ou modifiées. Nous leur indiquions *au préalable* les champs pour lesquels nous percevions des changements possibles.
>
> TT
> We *began* by notifying everyone via the Compendium's September newsletter to inform them of the project and to encourage them to validate the data files falling under their responsibility. *Then* we corresponded with the contact persons (or respondents, according to the situation) by telephone, e-mail or fax. We asked *them to* verify if the information describing the data in the files was still accurate and if any information had to be added or modified. We notified them *first* of which fields we felt possibly required changes.

The propositions in the paragraph are connected by a series of external temporal conjunctives. However, the translation of *au préalable* by *first* in the last sentence is confusing. The translator could have incorporated the last sentence in the penultimate sentence in order to clarify the sequence of events, as follows:

> We notified them of the fields that, in our opinion, might require changes and asked them to verify if the information describing the data in the files was still accurate and if any information had to be added or modified.

3.3.2. *Frequency and variety of conjunctives: a translation error case study*

The last example illustrates the use of several types of conjunctives within the same paragraph and the considerable problems that await the ill-prepared translator.

Subject: computer program for processing and displaying statistical data on cars, vans, and light trucks in Canada

> ST
>
> Le programme indiquera *également* un problème au niveau des marques JEEP qui n'apparaissent naturellement pas dans le dictionnaire des marques d'automobile. C'est *ainsi* qu'on a relevé plusieurs erreurs au niveau de la variable de l'ENUVeP qui indique le type du véhicule sélectionné afin de remplir le carnet d'achats de carburant. *En effet,* cette variable a été utilisée, au départ, dans le but de distinguer entre les voitures et les camions légers et de former deux fichiers traités séparément par le programme de fusion. *Or,* il s'est avéré dans certains cas qu'un type de véhicule mal spécifié avait entraîné le placement erroné d'un camion dans le fichier des voitures, comme l'illustre l'exemple précédent, ou vice versa. Une caractérisation adéquate dans les dictionnaires permet *donc* de valider certaines informations contenues dans les données d'enquête.
>
> TT
>
> The program will *also* indicate a problem of JEEP makes, which, naturally, is not in the dictionary of car makes. *In this way,* many errors were identified in the NaPVUS variable that indicate the type of vehicle selected to complete the fuel purchase diary. *In fact,* this variable was used, at the beginning, to differentiate between cars and light trucks and vans to form two files that are processed separately by the merge program. *It* turned out that, in some cases, a type of vehicle poorly specified led to the truck being poorly placed in the cars file, as illustrated in the preceding example, or vice versa. An adequately specified dictionary *therefore* allows certain information found in the study data to be authenticated.

While the first conjunctive (additive) is correctly rendered, the second (*ainsi,* additive) is slightly misinterpreted as an external causal, rather than an additive, and the third (*en effet*, additive) could be misinterpreted as an adversative by the reader. Non-translation of the additive *Or* is a valid solution for the third conjunctive. However, the fourth conjunctive (*donc*) is incorrectly rendered as an internal causal, whereas it is in fact a summarizing temporal and should have been translated by *in short* or *to sum up*.

What this short case study shows is that the conjunctive's role as an instruction is not sufficient to guide the reader through the text, because in many instances it can be interpreted variously, depending on the logical connection between two or more propositions. Thus Halliday and Hasan's contention that conjunctives do not in and of themselves create cohesion seems to be borne out. Their meaning and the cohesion relation are, in fact, activated by the reader, and by the translator, on the basis of their understanding of the surrounding propositions. Once again, the microtextual is contingent on the macrotextual.

3.3.3. *Other inference indicators*

Thomas defines a reasoned discourse as "any discourse in which some statement is given as a reason for some conclusion" (1986: 12). He goes on to list words and phrases that serve to indicate that one statement is being given as a reason for another; he calls them **inference indicators**. They include the causal conjunctives identified by Halliday and Hasan, but he adds a number of verb phrases and clauses that Joseph Williams categorizes, along with conjunctives, as the **metadiscourse** of writing, in that writers thereby refer to the act of writing or arguing by explicitly establishing a causal or other relationship between facts, events, or concepts (Williams 1990: 40). They are thus part of the narrative strategy to be discussed in greater detail in 3.10. They precede either reasons or conclusions (see example on p. 42).

Thomas contends that modal (auxiliary) verbs can be inference indicators too—for example, "Based on these facts, the event *must have occurred* in 1756." Here, the modal verb acts as a qualifier (modalizer) in the sense given the term in Toulmin's model. Some of the inference indicators listed above also act as qualifiers. There is, for example, a difference in force between "X *proves* that," on the one hand, and "X *suggests*" or "X *leads me to believe*," on the other.

Preceding reasons	*Preceding conclusions*
as shown by	this, which shows that
follows from	allows us to infer that
being that	suggest very strongly that
seeing that	proves that
assuming that	that
may be inferred from	you see that
may be derived from	it follows that
it is clear from	in this way we see that

Thomas points out that some reasoned discourse contains few, if any, inference indicators. Readers then have to base their understanding of the reasoning on propositional content alone. Inference indicators are nonetheless commonplace and, whether they are conjunctives, verb phrases, or clauses, contribute to establishing a chain of reasoning. Their omission or distortion can therefore be of significant consequence in a TQA context.

3.4. From inference indicators to propositional function

The next step in the modelling process is to establish linkages between conjunctives and other inference indicators and the higher-level argument structures described by Toulmin, Mendenhall, and other scholars. In other words, we have to find analytical tools enabling us to incorporate in the model the quality of *coherence* as the logical extension of *cohesion*.

Widdowson proposes a step-by-step procedure for determining and expressing the propositional development or chain of reasoning that gives a discourse its coherence. He uses inference indicators as a means of characterizing propositional development and suggests supplying one, where none exists, as a way of determining or clarifying the logical relationship between propositions. His model applies to all relationships between propositions, not just reason–conclusion pairs. He proposes a broad distribution of propositions into *theme* and *support* elements, which are then characterized according to what he calls their **illocutionary point** (function or purpose) within the discourse:

> **generalization** (main theme)
> **clarification** (introduced by additive conjunctives such as *for example* and *that is*)
> **elaboration** (introduced by additive conjunctives such as *in addition* and *moreover*)
> **consequence** (introduced by causal conjunctives such as *therefore* and *as a result*)
> **qualification** (introduced by adversative conjunctives such as *however* and *on the contrary*) (Widdowson 1978: 130–139)

I will add a function not explicitly stated by Widdowson, probably because it is closely related to clarification and consequence: *explanation*. In fact, it is the converse of consequence in that it serves to provide reasons for facts, events, and concepts. A typical conjunctive would be *for*, and all the inference indicators in Thomas's "preceding reasons" list (see 3.3.6) would signpost this function.

The following illustrates how Widdowson's models could be applied to translation analysis.

Example

The function type, in boldface and in brackets, follows the words it refers to. Explicit inference indicators are in italics; implicit ones are italicized within parentheses.

> Le Québec a connu en 1999 une croissance rapide **[generalization]**: (*plus précisément*) son produit intérieur brut (PIB) a progressé de 3,8 %, la deuxième meilleure performance de la décennie, ne le cédant que de peu à 1994 (+3,9 %) **[clarification]**. L'économie québécoise a *évidemment* [qualifier] bénéficié d'un environnement nord-américain très favorable : l'ensemble du pays a connu l'an dernier un rythme de croissance de 4,2 % égalant à cette occasion la progression enregistrée aux États-Unis **[explanation]**. Le Québec a *donc* connu encore une fois une croissance inférieure à celle de l'ensemble du pays **[consequence]**. *Toutefois*, si on tient compte de l'évolution de la population, on note que la progression per capita est la même au Québec que dans l'ensemble du Canada, ce qui vaut non seulement pour 1999 mais pour toute la période 1993-1999 **[qualification]**.

Widdowson represents propositional development graphically by means of an arrow diagram. Thus,

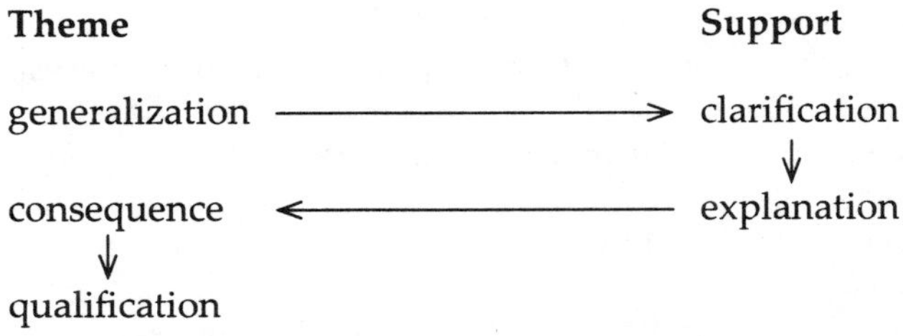

Translation of example

> **A rapidly expanding economy**
> In 1999, Quebec experienced rapid growth **[generalization]**: (*specifically*) the 3.8% rise in GDP was the province's second best performance of the decade, falling just short of the 1994 mark of 3.9% **[clarification]**. The Quebec economy *clearly* benefited from a very favourable North American environment: the 1999 growth rate for Canada as a whole was 4.2%, equalling that of the U.S. **[explanation]**. *Thus* Quebec's growth rate was once again below the national rate **[consequence]**. *However*, if we factor in population changes, we find that per capita growth in Quebec equals the national rate, both for 1999 and for the 1993–99 period as a whole **[qualification]**.

Incorporating this type of analysis into our model makes it possible to identify the various elements of the serial reasoning in a discourse—the elements that make it coherent. It is then possible to identify and explain text-level deficiencies in TT, as illustrated below in the analysis of a student's translation of an economics text.

Source text

> Longtemps abritée derrière ses frontières, la France exporte maintenant une partie extrêmement importante de sa richesse nationale **[generalization]** : (*plus précisément*) 40 % de sa production industrielle, 17 % de son produit intérieur brut **[clarification]**. *C'est assez dire* [inference indicator following reason] à quel point l'amélioration du niveau de vie des Français dépend maintenant des exportations de notre pays **[consequence]**.

Les économistes ont calculé cette dépendance **[generalization]**. (*Et*) Ils sont arrivés à la conclusion qu'à une croissance de 15 % environ de nos exportations cette année succéderait l'an prochain un progrès de 4 à 5 % seulement **[elaboration]**. (*Par ailleurs)* Ce chiffre tient compte de la réduction volontaire des exportations de produits intermédiaires à base de pétrole qu'il faudra opérer pour servir en priorité le marché intérieur **[elaboration]**. *C'est dire* [inference indicator following reason] *qu'*au lieu d'augmenter de quelque 24 milliards de francs en 1999, comme il était prévu, nos exportations (160 milliards de francs cette année, pour une richesse nationale de 1.000 milliards) ne croîtront que de 7 milliards **[consequence]**. Perte : 17 milliards **[consequence]**.

Le manque à gagner sera *en fait* plus important **[generalization/ elaboration]**. *Car* exportant moins, les chefs d'entreprise français investiront probablement moins, tandis que les particuliers consommeront également moins **[explanation]** *du fait* de la pénurie d'essence et d'une moindre amélioration de leur pouvoir d'achat **[explanation]**. La progression de la consommation des ménages pourrait *ainsi* revenir de 5,5 % cette année à 2,5 % ou 3 % seulement l'an prochain **[consequence]**.

Translation for assessment/revision and assessment in terms of propositional functions

After sheltering itself behind its borders for a long time, France now exports a large amount of its national wealth **[generalization]**: 40% of its industrial production *which is 17% of its gross domestic product* **[clarification error]**. Suffice to say the great degree the improvement in the standard of living of the French depends on France's exports **[elaboration]**.

Economists calculated this dependency and concluded that an increase this year of about 15% in our exports *would only create* a 4–5% improvement next year **[elaboration error]**. This figure takes into consideration an intentional reduction in exports of oil-based intermediate products that will first serve the domestic market **[elaboration]**.

Instead of increasing our exports by some 24 billion francs in 1999 as planned, (160 billion francs this year, for a national wealth of 1000 billion) they will only increase by 7 billion, resulting in a *loss* of 17 billion francs **[clarification error]**.

> The loss of *profit* will be, in fact more significant **[generalization error].** As a result of the *decrease* in exports **[clarification error],** French company owners will probably invest less **[consequence],** while individuals consume equally less, due to the gas shortage and a smaller improvement in purchasing power **[explanation].** The rise in household consumption could return *to* 5.5% this year and to 2.5 or 3% the next year **[consequence error]**.

Thus the analysis of propositional function immediately enables us to characterize most of the errors in terms of coherence and reasoning and to give characterization explanatory value.

3.5. Types of argument

3.5.1. Overview

According to both Ryan (1984) and Declerq (1993), an Aristotelian typology of arguments, or more properly reasoning, is based on the following criteria:

- Reasoning (argument) in science and mathematics is built on necessary, permanent premises, whereas reasoning (argument) in the social sciences, law, and the humanities is based on probable, debatable premises. The premises of science are those of physical states of affairs and are used to *demonstrate* a particular claim, which is considered *correct* or *incorrect*. The premises of law, politics, and other social sciences and humanities are those of human states of affairs and are used to *argue* for or against a particular claim, which is considered *acceptable* or *unacceptable*, *probable* or *improbable*. As I stated earlier, there is a significant body of literature attesting to the argumentative features of scientific writing. The broad distinction made above is nevertheless a useful starting point for a typology.
- Demonstration belongs to the realm of logic, argumentation to the realm of dialectic (structured argument between two parties; the art of critically investigating opinions) and rhetoric (art of persuasion through speech and, by extension, writing).

- We can therefore say that arguments have two functional components: a *logical* component, reflected in the pattern of reasoning and its validity, and an *ideological* component, reflected in the acceptability of the underlying values or beliefs to the readership. In addition, there is a third functional component, the *psychological* one, based on the emotional appeal of the speech or text and the relationship thus established between sender and receiver of the message. This third component of argumentation will be based on the sender's use of **ethos** (focus on moral image of sender) and **pathos** (appeal to emotions of receiver) to "win over" the receiver, and this is where a fourth component, the *aesthetic* one, comes into play in the form of figures. Arguments in scientific and nonscientific texts will embrace these components to varying degrees: in some, the logical component will dominate, with a claim being made and supported by a logical pattern of reasoning; in others, the psychological component will dominate, with a pattern of reasoning being combined with devices designed to appeal to the reader's or listener's emotions so as to ensure acceptance of the claim. For the evaluator, the manifestation of all four components in the source text would have to be rendered accurately in the target text for the translation to meet standards of adequacy.
- The structural basis of all reasoning and argument is the *syllogism*, comprising three parts—major premise, minor premise, and conclusion (claim). For example,

  Every broad-leafed plant is deciduous.
  Every vine is a broad-leafed plant.
  Therefore, every vine is deciduous.

  Particularly in nonscientific writing, the syllogism may be reduced to the *rhetorical syllogism*, or *enthymeme*, in which a commonly held belief or value is presupposed, not stated, but remains an integral part of the argument, or to an even more abbreviated form, the *maxim*. The ostensible reason for this brevity is that in order for the reader or listener to be persuaded, arguments must be lively, uncomplicated, and based on beliefs that he or she is familiar with and adheres to unquestioningly.

Enthymeme
[People require adequately funded health care to get well.]
People are being turned away from emergency departments.
Therefore, more money must be invested in health care.

Maxim
More investment in health care means fewer crises in Ontario's hospitals.

In much nonscientific writing—and, therefore, in nonscientific translation—major premises will always be commonly held beliefs or values: the overriding value of caring for the sick, the belief that smaller government is better government, and so on.

Whether expressed as syllogisms, enthymemes, or maxims, arguments fall into five broad categories or topics (lines of argument) in the theory of rhetoric: definition, comparison, relationship, circumstance, and testimony (Corbett and Connors 1999: 84–130). Such arguments may be developed throughout the text or within a paragraph or even a sentence. The examples below are necessarily short, and they do not cover all the possible subcategories, including those of false argument.

3.5.2. Definition

According to Corbett and Connors, the topic of definition can be used for clarifying a point at issue, suggesting a line of argument, or establishing a norm against which other propositions can be judged.

EXAMPLE

Text type: page on Web site of national organization
Purpose: to help young Canadians deal with dating, family, and friendship issues

> ST
> VIOLENCE AND RESPECT: Destruction of your personal property is a form of emotional abuse and potentially could lead to violence and physical abuse in your relationship. Please think about your personal property as a symbol of your personality. If someone attacks your property, they might as well be attacking you.

> TT
> VIOLENCE ET RESPECT : La destruction de vos biens est une forme de violence psychologique et pourrait conduire à de la violence physique dans votre relation. Considérez vos biens personnels comme étant le reflet de votre personnalité. Donc, en faisant violence à vos biens, on vous fait violence à vous.

In fact, there are two argumentative definitions in the ST, based on similarity: (1) destruction of personal property = form of violence; (2) personal property = symbol of personality. They are used as major and minor premises of a syllogism, the conclusion of which is the final proposition. The translation renders the syllogism adequately.

EXAMPLE

Text type: report on official languages situation in the Quebec region of a federal department
Purpose: to identify areas for improvement in services and staffing

> ST
> **Prestations de services bilingues aux employés**
> Une région désignée bilingue est un secteur géographique où les deux langues officielles sont habituellement utilisées, notamment en ce qui concerne la langue de travail. Dans les régions désignées bilingues, les employés ont le droit de travailler dans la langue officielle de leur choix sous réserve de servir le public. Ils ont droit à des instruments de travail, à des services centraux et personnels et à la supervision dans la langue de leur choix. Les réunions devraient se faire dans les deux langues.
>
> Régions bilingues prescrites au paragraphe 35(2) de la loi des langues officielles :
>
> Région de la capitale nationale
> La province du Nouveau-Brunswick
> La région bilingue de Montréal
> Les régions bilingues des « autres parties du Québec »
> La région bilingue de l'est de l'Ontario
> La région bilingue du nord de l'Ontario

> TT
> **Provision of bilingual services to employees**
> A designated bilingual region is a geographic sector where both official languages are normally used, particularly as languages of work. In designated bilingual regions, employees are entitled to work in the official language of their choice, subject to requirements regarding service to the public. They are entitled to receive work instruments, central services, personal services and supervision in the language of their choice. Meetings should be conducted in both official languages.
>
> Bilingual regions under section 35(2) of the Official Languages Act:
>
> National Capital Region
> Province of New Brunswick
> Bilingual region of Montreal
> Bilingual regions in other parts of Quebec
> Bilingual region of Eastern Ontario
> Bilingual region of Northern Ontario

This example illustrates the two types of argument from definition: genus and division. "Designated bilingual region" is defined, in the first paragraph, by certain qualities (genus) and, in the second, by its various components (division). On the surface, the writer seems to be stating a fact, not making an argument. Yet, in fact, it is because of the definitions that he can then affirm the rights of employees and the requirement for meetings to be conducted in both English and French. The translation renders the two definitions adequately.

In the examples, the definitions serve to set norms against which degree of violence in behaviour (in the first) and degree of service in both official languages (in the second) is to be assessed.

3.5.3. Comparison (similarity, difference, degree)

Identity (rule of justice)

"The rule of justice involves giving identical treatment to beings or situations of the same kind" (Perelman and Olbrechts-Tyteca, 1969: 218). This means reducing compared entities to those elements that are identical. The argument is particularly applicable in law, where the rule of justice calls for beings in the same essential category to be treated in the same way.

Example

Text type: letter
Purpose: to enlist education minister's support for the development of a curriculum in computer science for Francophones

> ST
> Il n'existe pas beaucoup d'outils en ce moment pour développer un curriculum complet en informatique. Nous avons un grand besoin de personnes compétentes en la matière pour voir au cheminement de ce dossier.
>
> Par contre, du côté anglophone, on a déjà une grande avance dans la création d'un curriculum en informatique. Il en est de même chez les autochtones. Le Ministre va-t-il nous accorder les mêmes droits?
>
> TT
> There are not many tools at this time to see to the development of a complete computer science curriculum. We have a great need of human resources who are competent in the subject to see to the furtherance of this matter.
>
> On the other hand, on the Anglophone side, they have already made great strides in the development of a computer science curriculum. It is the same situation with the Aboriginal peoples. Will the Minister give us the same rights?

The translation contains defects both of meaning and of language, but the argument is preserved. It is based on the equating of Francophones to Anglophones and Aboriginal people as linguistic groups; as such, Francophones deserve the same level of education programs.

Comparison (large/small)
Comparisons can be made by opposition (heavy/light), by ordering (heavier than), and by quantitative ordering (weight in terms of units). Arguments of this type are various and complex, and can range from statistical comparisons to ethical judgments. They serve to create an impression of unbiased reporting and objectivity.

EXAMPLE

Text type: report of survey of international students in Canada
Purpose: to publicize Canada's successes in international education and highlight areas for improvement

> ST
> While far from 100%, this number represents a doubling of the figure in the 1988 survey. Clearly we are doing something right—promotion, quality leading to positive word-of-mouth recommendations, etc.
>
> TT
> Bien que les réponses ne soient pas toutes favorables, le taux de satisfaction est deux fois plus élevé en 1999 qu'en 1988. Cela démontre clairement que certaines mesures au moins sont efficaces — la promotion porte des fruits, les étudiants étrangers recommandent à leurs amis de venir au Canada en raison de la qualité de nos programmes, etc.

The argument is based on the truism that the greater the statistical level of satisfaction is, the more effective the program is proven to be.

Example/illustration/analogy
The argument takes as its starting point a specific, known case and presents it as a precedent, a model for future action, or a general rule. It thus establishes reality on the basis of the individual case. "The latter can play a wide variety of roles: as an example, it makes generalization possible; as an illustration, it provides support for an already established regularity; as a model, it encourages imitation" (Perelman and Olbrechts-Tyteca, 1969: 350). As Toulmin et al. show (1984: 219), drawing general conclusions from the evidence of samples is an instance of argumentation by example. The illustration corroborates or promotes understanding of an established situation.

EXAMPLE

Text type: article in criminal justice
Purpose: discussion of challenges facing reparative justice

ST
Des concepts comme le pardon, la guérison, la réconciliation, la réparation des torts causés sont difficiles à définir. On ne peut prétendre y arriver par des voies simples. Au Québec, le dossier des Orphelins de Duplessis en est une bonne illustration. Ces hommes et ces femmes, placés dans des institutions ou des orphelinats en bas âge, ont dénoncé la violence et les abus dont certaines communautés religieuses se seraient rendues coupables à leur endroit. Ils ont réclamé des indemnisations et des excuses de la part des autorités religieuses et de l'État. Ce dossier a soulevé maintes questions et le débat est loin d'être réglé. Qui sont les victimes? Comment faire la preuve que de tels abus ont été commis et identifier les responsables? Comment évaluer les torts causés et quelles sont les limites d'une « juste réparation » ?

TT
Concepts like forgiveness, healing, reconciliation and repairing the harm done are difficult to define. There is no short and easy way of coming to grips with them. The Duplessis Orphans case is a good illustration. Men and women who had been placed in orphanages at a very young age spoke out about the violence they claimed to have suffered at the hands of certain religious orders. They demanded compensation and an apology from the religious authorities and the government. The case has raised a number of issues and it will be a while before it is settled. Who are the victims? How can it be proven that the abuse occurred? How can the perpetrators be identified? How does the system go about putting a value on the harm done and on "fair" reparation?

The Duplessis Orphans case illustrates a general, pre-established problem of definition. The illustration and its relationship with the problem are accurately rendered in the TT.

3.5.4. Relationship (cause and effect, contraries, contradiction)

Cause
This may take three broad forms: argumentation to (a) attach two successive events by means of a causal link; (b) reveal the existence of a potential cause of an event; and (c) show the effect that must result from a given event. The causal link established may be of fact to consequence or of end to means.

EXAMPLE

Text type: minister's message introducing ministry business plan
Purpose: publicize government's investment in health care

> ST
> Creating a modern health system has not been easy. But we are beginning to see the results and we will continue to make the necessary investments to create a better system for today and tomorrow. A strong economy supports and strengthens our commitment to the health system, allowing us to expand and improve access to all Ontarians.
>
> TT
> Édifier un système de santé moderne n'est pas tâche aisée, mais nous commençons à voir les résultats de notre travail et nous continuerons de faire les investissements nécessaires pour instaurer un meilleur système pour aujourd'hui et pour demain. Notre engagement envers le système de santé se trouve renforcé par la vigueur de l'économie actuelle, qui nous permet d'augmenter les services et d'améliorer l'accès pour tous les Ontariens et toutes les Ontariennes.

There is a chain of causal arguments at work here. The most explicit one involves an end (better health-care system) and means (reform and investment). The second one, also explicit, involves cause and effect—a strong economy makes more investment in health care possible. But embedded in the statement is another end–means relationship—it is the government's action that has strengthened the economy in the first place, creating the conditions for renewed investment in health. The translation accurately reflects the argument structure.

Sign
Arguing from sign is a cause argument of particular relevance to science (symptoms, physical evidence) and law (physical and circumstantial evidence).

EXAMPLE

Text type: environmental inspection report
Purpose: to assess environmental risk

ST
Site No. A471403 did not show any signs of leachate springs. However, the surface water runoff collected in the north perimeter ditch of site No. A471403 discharges into a natural depression between the Rigaud River and the east toe of both sites. Part of the depression located on site No. 471402 was filled with waste which obstructs the natural flow of the water. The water collected up-gradient eventually seeps through the waste and discharges directly into the Rigaud River, which most likely contains leachate parameters.

TT
Le lieu d'enfouissement nº A471403 ne présente aucun signe de pollution des eaux souterraines par du lixiviat. Toutefois, les eaux de ruissellement qui s'accumulent au périmètre nord du lieu d'enfouissement nº A471403 finissent par se déverser dans une dépression naturelle située entre la rivière Rigaud et la limite est des deux lieux d'enfouissement. La dépression située au lieu nº A471402 était partiellement remplie de déchets qui obstruaient l'écoulement naturel des eaux de ruissellement. Les eaux provenant du haut de la pente finissent par traverser les déchets et aboutissent dans la rivière Rigaud, qui renferme tout probablement des polluants associés au lixiviat.

While the first sentence of the ST states that there is no sign of actual pollution, the rest of the text is a description of physical conditions normally indicating the presence of pollution. The TT accurately reflects the argument.

3.5.5. *Circumstance (possibility, past fact/future fact)*

This type of argument involves claiming that if a particular set of facts, events, or circumstances is possible, so can another, or that if a particular thing occurred in the past, another thing can occur in the future.

Part/whole
There are two groups of arguments here: (a) comparison of the whole to one of its parts, based on the principle that what is possible for the whole is also possible for the part; (b) division of the whole into its parts, based on the principle that what does not belong to any part cannot belong to the whole and that anything to be claimed for the whole must be established for one of the parts.

EXAMPLE

Text type: letter to minister
Purpose: request higher lumber production quota

> ST
> Notre scierie demande donc l'octroi d'un quota équitable par rapport à l'ensemble de l'industrie de sciage au Québec. Globalement, l'attribution des contingents au Québec est de 3,8 MMpmp pour une production québécoise de 7,0 MMpmp, soit plus de 54 %.
>
> À 54 % de sa production, le quota alloué à notre compagnie sous le régime de base (RB) devrait être de 40 000 Mpmp. Notre volume d'attribution étant actuellement de 11 635 Mpmp, la part manquante s'établira à 28 365 Mpmp à partir du 1er avril 1999.
>
> TT
> Accordingly, our sawmill is asking for a fair quota equivalent to the average for the Quebec sawmill industry as a whole. The Quebec quota is 3.8 MMFBM out of a total production of 7.0 MMFBM, or over 54%.
>
> A 54% basic-system quota for our company should generate 40,000 MFBM, compared with a current volume of 11,635 MFBM. Thus without a change in our quota, our shortfall will be 28,365 MFBM as of April 1, 1999.

The writer is arguing that the part (sawmill) should benefit from the same treatment that the whole (all similar industries in Quebec) receives. The translation accurately reflects the argument.

Means/end

EXAMPLE

Text type: self-protection training manual for persons with disabilities
Purpose: to inform consumers of safety and security risks and how to deal with them.

> ST
> The simplest precautions prove the most valuable. A small initial outlay will, in many cases, make our home or place of residence much more secure and buy peace of mind in the bargain.

> TT
> Et ce sont les précautions les plus simples qui sont les plus efficaces. En général, c'est en dépensant une petite somme pour la sécurité au départ que nous rendrons notre maison ou appartement beaucoup plus sûr et que nous pourrons assurer en même temps notre tranquillité d'esprit.

The argument from circumstance is that, if the means (money, will) to do something is present, it (greater security) can be done. The argument is combined with an argument from comparison by degree. The translation is adequate.

3.5.6. *Testimony (authority, testimonial, law, precedent, statistics, maxim)*

Authority
This involves an appeal to a person's or group's reputation in order to justify a claim.

EXAMPLE

Text type: discussion paper on criminal justice
Purpose: presentation of challenges to social reintegration of inmates

> ST
> L'attitude du public face aux contrevenants a plutôt tendance à être revancharde, punitive et impatiente. [...]
> Déplorer cette attitude du public, dénoncer le fait qu'elle est mal fondée et qu'elle conduit ainsi tout droit vers des problèmes sociaux encore plus graves, en pointer du doigt les conséquences, voilà autant d'observations qui sont d'ores et déjà devenues les nouveaux lieux communs de la criminologie canadienne. Il ne fait aucun doute que notre société, parce qu'elle a eu récemment tendance à écouter davantage sa peur que son courage ou sa compassion, s'est engagée sur un chemin dangereux.
>
> TT
> [The general public] generally takes a vengeful, punitive, impatient attitude toward offenders. [...]
> Statements deploring the public's attitude, condemning the fact that it is unfounded and is a direct cause of even more serious

> social problems and highlighting the consequences, are now commonplace in Canadian criminology literature. It is true that our society has in recent years tended to react with fear rather than courage and compassion and has consequently embarked on a dangerous course [...].

Note that the authority is not a specific piece of research or researcher but recently published Canadian criminology research results as a whole, which lend even more force to the criticism of public attitudes. The translation accurately renders the argument.

As the examples above show, many types of argument are present not only in the more polemical fields of politics and law but also in other areas of instrumental translation, including criminology, administration, psychology, and environmental protection. It is my premise that assessment of the transfer of such arguments should be not only an integral but also a key part of a full-text TQA system, *since each argument lies at the core of text content and determines the reader's response to the text*. To use the terminology of speech act theory, the argument is a prime **perlocutionary** device, designed to elicit a specific response, be it acceptance, understanding, support, a change of policy, or another response.

3.6. Figures

3.6.1. Overview

The third component of rhetoric in our tentative TQA model is that of figures of speech. Figures tend to be microtextual: they are created most often at the subsentence and subparagraph level, although some may operate at the discourse level, as in the case of analogy and irony. On the basis of the analysis by Dubois et al. (1970), a figure can be described as a deliberate deviation ("écart," as opposed to "erreur") from the conventional meaning or form of language. Figures have traditionally been treated as a matter of stylistics and aesthetics, but the New Rhetoric has shown the important role they play in argumentation proper, if certain conditions are met:

> We consider a figure to be *argumentative*, if it brings about a change in perspective, and its use seems normal in relation to this new situation. If, on the other hand, the speech does not bring about the adherence

> of the hearer to this argumentative form, the figure will be considered an embellishment, a figure of style. (Perelman and Olbrechts-Tyteca 1969: 169)

In other words, if the perlocutionary effect of the figure prevails over the hearer's or reader's perception of it as a device, it is an argumentative tool.

It has been demonstrated that figures are part and parcel of writing in the natural sciences, mathematics, social sciences, and the humanities; they contribute to the rhetorical effect, or persuasiveness, of the argument or demonstration being presented. For example, Angenot (1982) shows how they are combined with, or actually function as, enthymemes and maxims to form arguments in polemical documents (pamphlets). Saragossi (1991), in her wide-ranging discourse analysis of a corpus of political speeches originating in the Department of External Affairs of Canada (now called the Department of Foreign Affairs and International Trade), identifies a host of types of figures that contribute to the persuasive intentions of the writer: euphemism (to downplay, even eliminate from discourse a threat to economic stability), enallage (shift from "I" to "we" to minimize distance between sender and receiver of message), antithesis (industrialization/natural resources, developing countries/industrialized countries), rhetorical question (to make appearance pass for fact), synecdoche (belief justifying action), prolepsis (countering anticipated criticisms), antonomasia (periphrasis), epanorthosis (rectification of preceding statement to reveal true intentions), preterition (referring to a subject while maintaining that one will not talk about it), and others. Following in Angenot's footsteps, Saragossi establishes links between figures and various types of argument, but she also brings out the synergy between figures and speech acts. Through figures, the act of assertion can subtly be transformed into a directive or commissive act, persuading the receiver of the message to act or guaranteeing a positive resolution of a situation at some future time. McCloskey (1985) establishes a similar list of rhetorical figures in the science of economics. In fact, there is such a plethora of devices in the modern economics textbook, says McCloskey, that economics, far from adhering to the scientism and positivist approach that it claims for itself, "is a collection of literary forms. Indeed, science is a collection of literary forms, not a science. And literary forms are scientific" (1985: 55).

In incorporating figures into the model, we must categorize them in a way that will be helpful for assessment. Dubois et al. and, later,

Corbett and Connors distinguish between figures of content (logical and semantic elements), or **tropes**, and figures of expression (morphology, syntax, graphology), or schemes. We can assume that most of the figures in instrumental translation will be of the former type and we will focus on them. They will more often than not be examples of what Dubois et al. call "metalogism," or manipulation of logical relations (litotes, hyperbole, repetition, pleonasm, antithesis, euphemism, irony, paradox, etc.). Metalogisms are translatable (Dubois et al. 1970: 132), unlike many other types of figures. Semantic figures ("metasememes" in Dubois's terminology) include synecdoche, simile, metaphor, metonymy, and oxymoron.

3.7. Narrative strategy

The way in which the narrator (I extend the use of the term here to all types of instrumental texts) reveals or hides his or her "presence" in the text is part of argumentation strategy.

3.7.1. Depersonalization

Narrative strategy can take several forms. The "depersonalization" of the narrator as a means of projecting objectivity in scientific texts is well documented. Indeed, it helps to create the illusion that the content is not argumentative but a straightforward recounting of facts, and it is thus a rhetorical device. As McGuire and Melia point out, "It is through this depersonalization that the experimental or theoretical paper possesses its fundamental characteristic, that of being a *report*" (1989: 87). It is as if the "facts speak for themselves," and accordingly the (supposedly) diminished authorial role is often combined with diminished authorial responsibility (in the cognitive sense) for the content of the document: "The desubjectivation that results measurably reduces *real* authorial control and manipulation over *meaning*" (1989: 96). Because the text is depersonalized, the "facts" are there for all experts to examine and come to a consensus (or dissensus) about. The authors see in this important lessons for rhetoric in general: "The strategy of normatively "depersonalizing" a scientific text is a deliberately rhetorical move. Indeed, in the very process of minimizing those literary features that carry rhetorical nuance, the scientific community establishes a positive rhetoric for disguising the rhetorical" (1989: 96).

Depersonalization and desubjectivation take many forms: using the passive voice, making nouns for activities and documents the subjects of statements ("Studies show"; "X's report states"), and making the narrator the object of the statement ("The results seemed plausible to us"). These devices are commonplace in a broad range of instrumental texts, so I propose to examine their role in argumentation and their treatment in translations of nonscientific material.

The presence of depersonalization in fields other than scientific ones is demonstrated by Greimas (1983). He examines the phenomenon with reference not to the natural sciences but to research documents in the humanities and social sciences, showing how depersonalization and desubjectivation serve to create an "objective discourse" designed to mask, to some extent, the writer's (researcher's) production of knowledge ("performances cognitives") in the guise of facts to be discovered (1983: 188–89, 196–97). The writer's ultimate objective is, of course, to *persuade* the reader of the "veracity" of the discourse.

Greimas lists several depersonalization devices:

- reference to other researchers' work ("depuis Darmesteter," "après MM. B. Geiger et H. Lommel")
- nominalization in place of subject + verb ("effort … qui n'a pas abouti")

At the same time, Greimas notes that the narrator is not completely removed from the text as subject. He illustrates this fact with examples such as "Nous nous sommes proposé d'étudier" and "Nous avons dû … examiner" (1983: 182). This "cognitive" level of discourse does not, however, conflict with the "objective" level; rather, the different forms of cognitive activity contribute to the narrative structure of the text as a report (étudier→examiner→préciser les rapports …).

The absence of the subject per se is not the only factor in analyzing the narrative strategy as an integral part of argumentation strategy. Ouellet (1984; 1985; 1992) refers to a wide variety of other means of prompting the reader to enter into a contract with the writer and accept the veracity of his or her statements in scientific discourse. Depersonalization—or what Ouellet calls "désénonciation" (1985: 50)—is created by means of a number of morphosyntactic structures:

- *Deverbalization/nominalization*
  La culture de *Mucor hiemalis* (<J'ai cultivé …)

- *Passive voice instead of agent and active voice*
  L'éthylidène est isolé
- *Use of the participle (adjective)*
  L'éthylidène isolé
- *Modalization*
  L'éthylidène peut être isolé
- *Use of reflexive verb form*
  L'éthylidène s'isole
  (Ouellet 1992: 416)

For Ouellet, each morphosyntactic device serves to shift the point of view on the "fact" in question, concealing the real agent, making the patient ("éthylidène") the apparent agent, turning process into fact (nominalization), or modifying the process (modal verb). In other words, the narrative strategy involves controlling how "facts" are shown and therefore how they are perceived.

The above devices all help to create an objective discourse, which is then interspersed with modal expressions or qualifiers. In this way, the text communicates to the reader, as objective facts, evaluative judgments made by the writers and not supported, explicitly, by hard facts. The ways in which these judgments are expressed are a key part of the "argumentative program" of the text.

Examples from scientific texts on mushrooms cited by Ouellet (1984: 38):

> La croissance en anaérobiose... est un phénomène *plus* commun *que*...
> ... à part les levures, *quelques* champignons appartenant *principalement* aux genres...
> ... des modifications *importantes* de la synthèse des stérols...
> ... l'anaérobiose influence la synthèse des stérols *mais aussi, et de façon très profonde,* la morphologie des cellules...
> ... c'est *toutefois* la synthèse des stérols qui *semble la plus affectée* par l'anaérobiose...

The italicized words and phrases communicate the narrator's "objective" interpretation of the evidence. Note in the last item that depersonalization (objectivity) is combined with an argumentative operator (*toutefois*): depersonalization and desubjectivation serve to present the author's interpretation as an account of objective relations between phenomena, as if the adversative connection resided in those phenomena. At the same time, the scientific process itself is personified, becoming the subject of an action ("l'anaérobiose influence ...").

In the end, all these morphosyntactic devices of depersonalization conceal a multitude of speech acts, particularly assertive ("I find that, I conclude that") and evaluative ("I consider these changes important"). Their concealment is an integral part of the process of persuading the reader of the veracity of the statements made through a gradual change in the "speaker" of scientific discourse. Ouellet identifies four steps:

- the presentation of "they-the facts" as agent ("la culture de l'anaérobiose");
- the replacement of the "I" of the real subject (narrator/author/researcher) with the "we" of the subject together with the reader who buys into the contract. Perelman and Olbrechts-Tyteca (1969: 178) consider this device a figure, calling it "enallage of person";
- the shift from the "we" to the scientific community or to science itself ("they");
- once the "factual" nature of the findings is established, introduction of the scientist-narrator at the end of the discourse through various deictics (*nous, ce travail, ici,* etc.).

In fact, we can establish a direct relationship between depersonalization—the shift from the subject to the scientific community, science, and the facts as narrative force—and the argument schema assembled by Toulmin. For it is science and the facts that provide the warrant and backing for authorial claims. Yet the facts *do not* speak for themselves; to make them appear to do so is to engage in rhetoric and argumentation.

Thus depersonalization (or personalization) ties in with full-text TQA and specifically with argumentation-centred assessment. It is an integral part of the arsenal of techniques of persuasion at the writer's disposal, and failure to render it appropriately may well have an adverse effect on the degree of persuasiveness of the translation. It will be interesting to determine to what extent the technique is present in nonscientific texts and whether it is a factor in the quality of translations of those texts.

3.7.2. *Qualifiers*

Depersonalization is not the only narrative strategy at work in instrumental texts. McCloskey refers to the technique of scientific modesty whereby economists mitigate their assertions—for example, "I would like to suggest," "it seems" and "as a first approximation"—or reinforce them—for example, "is beyond dispute" and "we make the critical assertion that ..." In both cases, the qualifying elements function at the psychological level of argument, conveying an image of the economist as a person of caution or of conviction, and therefore to be believed. Note, however, that qualifiers can also take the form of adjectives and adverbs, as Ouellet has cogently illustrated.

3.8. Argumentation parameters and TQA grid

Adding organizational relations, propositional functions, conjunctives, and other inference indicators, argument types, figures, and narrative strategy to argument schema, we now have a multi-parameter grid for argumentation-centred TQA.

Core Argumentation Parameters

Argument schema	Claims, grounds, etc.
Arrangement/organizational relations	Problem–solution, conclusion–reason, etc.
Propositional functions/ conjunctives/other inference indicators	Clarification, elaboration, consequence, etc.; additive, adversative, causal, temporal; preceding reasons, preceding conclusions
Arguments	Definition, comparison, relationship, etc.
Figures of speech	Tropes: metaphor, rhetorical question, etc.
Narrative strategy	Depersonalization, etc.

The fact that the qualifier/modalizer operates both as a component of the argument schema and as a part of narrative strategy is important for three reasons. First, far from being an accessory, it is an important, integral part of discourse. Second, it illustrates the synergy between the elements of rhetorical topology and the argument schema, between microtext and the text as a whole. Third, it reinforces my contention that any element of the argument structure may be integral to the argument schema, may therefore be an essential part of the text, and may therefore be the locus of an error of transfer of the core argument. The resulting TQA grid looks like this:

Argumentation-Centred TQA Grid

Element	Translation assessment
Argument schema	
Arrangement/ organizational relations	
Propositional functions/ conjunctives/ other inference indicators	
Arguments	
Figures	
Narrative strategy	

The advantage of the argument structure and TQA grid presented in the preceding tables is that *they cover all aspects of the messages(s) and purpose of a text. They bear on the full text, the microtext, and their interdependencies. As such, they meet a key criterion of TQA validity: measurement of a sufficient quantity of the object of evaluation so that the results—assuming validity of the other features of the model—may be applicable to the object as a whole.*

CHAPTER FOUR

DEFINING MAJOR ERROR, TESTING THE MODEL, AND DETERMINING THE QUALITY STANDARD: PREPARATORY STEPS

4.1. Defining major error

Experts in industrial quality control (ICQ) systems have generally broken down errors—more properly termed "defects" in the ICQ field—into three types by degree of gravity: critical, major, and minor. An authoritative U.S. manual gives the following definitions:

> CRITICAL DEFECT. A critical defect is a defect that judgment and experience indicate is likely to result in hazardous or unsafe conditions for individuals using, maintaining, or depending on the product; or a defect that judgment and experience indicate is likely to prevent performance of the tactical function of a major item such as a ship, aircraft, tank, missile or space vehicle.
>
> MAJOR DEFECT. A major defect is a defect, other than critical, that is likely to result in failure, or reduce materially the usability of the unit of product for its intended purpose.
>
> MINOR DEFECT. A minor defect is a defect that is not likely to reduce materially the usability of the unit of product for its intended purpose, or is a departure from established standards having little bearing on the effective use or operation of the unit.
> (Hayes and Romig, 1982: 146)

"Generally speaking," says Japanese expert Ishikawa, "one can never allow a critical defect, but a small number of minor defects is acceptable" (1985: 51). The critical defect affects life and safety. A major defect prevents the proper functioning of a product, as in the case of a car engine that does not work. In other words, both critical and major defects have significant adverse consequences for the end user. A minor defect such as a few scratches on a car does not impair operation, though it may not be appreciated by the prospective buyer.

How we can relate these concepts to TQA? Critical defects could occur in scientific and technical translations, such as assembly and operating manuals and medical procedures. Even in the social sciences, errors in translating quantities (in financial documents) could be deemed critical depending on the potential financial damage. Errors in legal translation could have severe financial or legal consequences for the parties concerned. Generally, however, serious translation errors bear not on life, safety, or the operation of a "major item" but on the usability of the text. Hence TQA systems have tended to merge critical and major defects into one category, the "major" error.

So at what point does an error "reduce materially the usability" of a translation? The Canadian government's Translation Bureau defines a major error of meaning as "the complete failure to render the meaning of a word or group of words conveying an essential part of the message." Indeed, it is reasonable to assume that not all parts of a translation are equally important and that, in many instances, certain specific sections convey the core argument or message of the ST and must be rendered appropriately in the TT. Provided that those essential parts of the text are translated accurately, the translation is usable, notwithstanding intrinsically serious errors elsewhere in the document. In fact, errors elsewhere would be deemed minor, whatever the degree of failure to convey the message. Note also that language errors in an essential portion of a text can be major too—for example, repetition of a rudimentary error (several spelling errors or punctuation errors, assessed as one major error) in a document for publication or a public sign.

The problem is how to define "essential."

To resolve the problem, while retaining the criterion of usability, I suggest that misinterpretation of the nodes of Toulmin's argument schema (backing, warrant, grounds, claim, rebuttal, and even, in some cases, qualifier/modalizer) constitutes major error and renders a translation undeliverable without revision, for the schema conveys the core argument of the whole text and is not confined to one, albeit essential, part. Using Toulmin's model as our reference point, we have a theoretical, rather than empirical, framework for determining what is "essential" in a text.

Therefore, in applying the argumentation-centred TQA model to some test cases, we will also explore the validity of defining major/critical error as a component not of "*an* essential part of the message" but of "*the* core argument" of the document and of proving the following:

> *If there are no defects at the level of the argument schema, the text meets minimum quality standards, since the elements of the core argument [BWGQCR] are the only potential loci of major or critical errors.*

We will examine the usefulness of maintaining the critical/major/minor error categories, reserving the "critical" designation for argument schema defects and "major" for serious defects at a lower level. We will use the term "defect" for argumentation-related errors. Hatim and Mason have already proposed (1997: 203) that the word "error" be restricted to overt microtextual errors of denotation and target-language errors of grammar, usage, and typography.

4.2. Testing the model

The preliminary TQA grid is tested on a small group of instrumental texts:

a) two Canadian government statistics/energy texts
b) two popular criminology/legal issues texts

I selected unrevised translations so as to ensure some level of uniformity in conditions of production. I also ensured that the texts were of varying length so that we could conduct our comparative analysis of microtextual and macrotextual approaches to TQA.

The popular criminology texts are argumentative, even polemical, and will therefore afford us ample opportunity to test the full range of parameters. On the other hand, the statistics documents are not at all polemical, and as such they will give us an opportunity to determine whether an argumentation-centred TQA model is of any use in a more "technical" field.

4.3. Determining the translation quality standard

My assumption is that identification and appropriate rendering of the argument (reasoning) schema is the key to meeting the translation quality standard, as opposed to the laws, rules, conventions, and norms that have been the focus of functionalist theory. We will explore the concepts of **validity** and **reliability** of translation standards with reference to general quality-control research and use the findings and conclusions reached in our application of argumentation-centred TQA parameters and major errors to determine the characteristics of a specific set of translation quality standards.

PART II

TESTING AND REFINING THE MODEL AND DEFINING A QUALITY STANDARD

CHAPTER FIVE

TESTING THE MODEL

5.1. Analytical process

Following the approach developed in chapter three, I start my analysis of each text by establishing the ST argument schema, arrangement, and organizational relations. This should enable us to identify, among other things, what part or parts of the document contain "essential messages"—that is, one or more of the components of Toulmin's argument schema.

The second stage of the analysis will be an examination of the TT without reference to the original to assess overall coherence and identify any potential problems within the core passages (containing schema elements). As mentioned in chapter one, this stage is part of the Ontario Government Translation Services procedure (1.1.1), and, in the case of student translations, Adab proposes an initial reading and even grading of the complete target text "as a TL (target language) text, for coherence and overall acceptability/readability" (2000: 224). So we will in fact be testing the assumption that a reading of the TT, prior to any comparative analysis, is useful for a textological, and specifically argumentation-centred, approach to TQA.

Subsequent stages involve assessment of TT against ST in relation to the argumentation parameters outlined in the last chapter: argument schema, arrangement/organizational relations; prepositional functions and conjunctives/other inference indicators; types of arguments; figures of speech (tropes); and narrative strategy.

At the end of the process, we make an overall argumentation-centred TQA based on the evidence accumulated thus far and compare the results with those of quantitative-microtextual TQA, using Sical and GTS (see 1.1.1) as reference points.

At this stage, the proposed procedure will seem intensive and time-consuming, but my purpose is to explain and demonstrate the model, for which I will use the acronym ARTRAQ. Actual ARTRAQ assessment in the field would, of course, drop much of the explanation and detail given below.

Summary of Analysis and Demonstration Process

1.	Establish argument schema/arrangement/organizational relations of ST and core passage(s)
2.	Read whole TT for potential problems of coherence, with particular reference to core passage(s), and determine whether overall arrangement is preserved or appropriately modified
3.	Conduct TQA of core passages to determine degree to which they reflect argument schema/arrangement/organizational relations, as required
4.	Conduct comparative assessment of propositional functions/conjunctives and other inference indicators
5.	Conduct comparative assessment of arguments
6.	Conduct comparative assessment of figures of speech (tropes)
7.	Conduct comparative assessment of narrative strategy
8.	Make overall quality statement on the basis of argumentation-centred TQA and compare results with those of quantitative, microtextual TQA

5.2. Analysis

A characterization of each microtextual error detected in the translation is inserted in parentheses immediately following the error in the TT. The symbols T (translation/transfer error) and L (target language error) have been used for this purpose. Samples of 400 words (typical sample length) are marked off with square bullets.

5.2.1. Translations of statistics texts for the Canadian government

In order to demonstrate the applicability of the model to a range of specialties, we begin with texts in the field of statistics, where, one might assume, factual information and objective mathematical analysis would predominate at the expense of value-based argument.

The selected texts were translated by a private company for Natural Resources Canada. One of the department's branches, the Office of Energy Efficiency, administers or has access to a number of databases containing information of various kinds on vehicles, driving patterns, and vehicle energy consumption. The databases are the source of periodic statistical studies on vehicle use and fuel efficiency. Translations of study reports and related documents are under consideration here.

The translations discussed below are drafts submitted by freelance translators for revision before delivery to the client.

Text 1

Title: (ST) *Fusion des données de l'Enquête nationale sur l'utilisation des véhicules privés et des taux de consommation de carburant estimés en laboratoire par les manufacturiers* / (TT) *Merger of data from National Private Vehicle Use Survey and Manufacturers' Laboratory-tested Fuel Consumption Rates*

ST length: 14,000 words
Text type: statistical report focusing on methodology used
Text mode: explanatory (how data merger program was constructed)
Purpose: present the methodology of a project to merge data from two databases—the National Private Vehicle Use Survey (NaPVUS) and the Manufacturers' Laboratory-tested Fuel Consumption Rates—and, especially, explain how the numerous discrepancies between the two databases and data sets were resolved
Translation purpose: same as ST

1. *Argument schema/arrangement/organizational relations*
Because of the length of the document, we summarize below what Andrews (1995) calls the "syntagmatic arrangement" of the content in order to gauge what broad patterns of reasoning and logical organization are at play.

What emerges is a painstaking process of elimination of all observations containing missing or erroneous values that could distort the calculations from the merger. The writer also builds on the initial descriptions of the two databases and the five main variables of interest, refining the data values constantly as she works toward as close a match of variable definitions as possible. The reader therefore needs to understand and retain all steps in the definition and refinement process.

The arrangement is therefore both chronological and logical, both conjunctive and hierarchical (Mendenhall 1990: 49), with each part of the operation necessarily following the preceding one to ensure achievement of the objective stated in the introduction.

Arrangement

1. **Introduction**: statement of purpose of merger, which will revolve around five key variables: model year, make, model, number of cylinders, and transmission type
2. **Preliminary processing procedures for each database**:
   - Process for eliminating certain observations
   - Arrangement of data to facilitate match with the other database, e.g., division of observations in one database into cars and light trucks/vans, as in the other database
   - Program for correcting erroneous observations
3. **Merger**: five steps based on five variables of interest; special cases
4. **Refinement of merger**
5. **Calculation of average fuel consumption ratio (AFCR)**: values and observations eliminated and variables representing calculations
6. **Calculation of average vehicle weight (AVW)**: values and observations eliminated and variables representing calculations
7. **Variables created by merger operation**: list of values and definitions of variables

Argument Schema

Element	**Description**
Claim	Successful merger of two data sets, with resulting ability to calculate laboratory-tested average fuel consumption ratios and average vehicle weights
Grounds	Procedures involved in preparing for, implementing, and refining the merger
Backing	Computer programming and statistical rules, formulas, and methods
Warrant	Scientism — belief in effectiveness and accuracy of science and scientific systems
Qualifier	N/A
Rebuttal/ restriction	Restrictions on use of many observations because of missing or erroneous values

Organizational relations: The binary structure may be viewed in two ways—as goal (calculation of AFCR and AVW)/means (merger operation) and as process (merger)/stage (each operation).

2. *Reading of TT*
Numerous target language shortcomings were noted, including typos and poorly constructed sentences that were difficult to follow. In several instances, the logical development of argument between sentences is unclear. Examination of TT also shows that few, if any, parts of the document are immaterial to its semantic core. All passages contain elements of the process (grounds) or target calculations (claims). All samples would therefore contain "essential" messages of ST.

I have selected a portion of the text in which problems of syntax and clarity have been identified.

> SOURCE TEXT
>
> **Traitement préliminaire des marques et modèles**
> Un traitement préliminaire des variables marque (MAKE) et modèle (MODEL), afin d'uniformiser les contenus de ces deux variables caractères, a été réalisé à l'aide de programmes en langage PERL. Ces programmes interactifs corrigent, à l'aide de dictionnaires prédéfinis par l'utilisateur, les erreurs de frappe dans les entrées de ces deux variables. De plus, les programmes corrigent les valeurs aberrantes de l'une ou l'autre de ces entrées. Lorsqu'il ne reconnaît pas une marque ou un modèle n'apparaissant pas dans le dictionnaire correspondant, le programme PERL demande à l'usager s'il souhaite procéder à la correction de la marque ou du modèle en question. Dans l'affirmative, le programme inscrit les corrections de marque ou de modèle suggérées par l'utilisateur. À partir de ce moment, le programme tiendra compte de ces nouvelles modifications qui seront alors ajoutées au dictionnaire pour toutes ses corrections futures.
> ■ Par exemple, le programme corrigeant les marques de voitures indiquera une erreur typographique dans une entrée de marque « Chervolet ». Une fois cette entrée remplacée par « Chevrolet », toutes les entrées suivantes comportant le même type d'erreur seront automatiquement corrigées, sans faire appel à nouveau au consentement de l'usager. Le programme offre également une option permettant de modifier à la fois la marque et le modèle. Cette option, dont il a été fait usage uniquement pour les données

d'enquête, a permis de corriger certaines imprécisions quant à la marque et au modèle du véhicule sélectionné, tels qu'ils ont été spécifiés par le répondant. À titre d'illustration, dans l'ENUVeP pour l'un des trois trimestres de 1996, une des personnes sondées a répondu, pour la marque et le modèle du véhicule sélectionné, « Sable » et « Mercury », respectivement. Le programme corrigeant les marques identifie alors une erreur au niveau de « Sable » qui n'apparaît pas dans le dictionnaire des marques. L'usager, constatant l'inversion qui s'est produite entre les noms de marque et de modèle, pourra alors corriger cette erreur.

Le programme signalera également un problème au niveau des marques JEEP, qui n'apparaissent évidemment pas dans le dictionnaire des marques d'automobiles. C'est ainsi qu'on a relevé plusieurs erreurs au niveau de la variable de l'ENUVeP qui indique le type du véhicule sélectionné afin de remplir le carnet d'achats de carburant. En effet, cette variable a été utilisée, au départ, dans le but de distinguer entre les voitures et les camions légers afin de former deux fichiers traités séparément par le programme de fusion. Or, il s'est avéré dans certains cas qu'un type de véhicule mal spécifié avait entraîné le placement erroné d'un camion dans le fichier des voitures, comme l'illustre l'exemple précédent, ou vice versa. Une caractérisation adéquate dans les dictionnaires permet donc de valider certaines informations contenues dans les données d'enquête. Enfin, il est possible, grâce à l'un ou l'autre des programmes et à l'aide des dictionnaires définis en fonction des marques et des modèles répertoriés dans la banque de données VFEES, de repérer des combinaisons erronées de marques et de modèles. Ces dernières, ne permettant pas d'identifier convenablement la marque et le modèle du véhicule, ont dû être éliminées du processus de fusion. ■

TARGET TEXT

Preliminary processing of makes and models

A preliminary processing of the variables MAKE and MODEL, *(L—comma splice)* to standardize the contents of these two characteristic variables was completed using programs written in Perl (Practical Extraction and Report Language). These interactive programs correct, with the help of dictionaries predefined by the user, the typographical errors in the entries for these two variables.

Furthermore, the programs correct the deviant *(T—terminology)* values in these entries. When the software *(T—change of subject)* recognizes *(Major T—contradiction)* a make or model that is not in the corresponding dictionary, the Perl program asks the user if he or she would like to correct the make or model in question. If yes, the program records the corrections to the make or model suggested by the user. From this moment on, the program will take into account the new modifications, which are added to the dictionary for any future occurrences of this error.

■ For example, the program correcting the makes of vehicles would indicate that there is a typographical error for the make entry "Chervolet." Once this entry is replaced with the correct spelling of "Chevrolet," each entry that follows with the same type of error will be automatically corrected, without asking the user. The program also has an option that allows the make and model to be corrected at the same time. This option, which was used only for the study *(T—mistranslation)* data, allowed certain inaccuracies concerning the make and model of the selected vehicle, as specified by the respondent, to be detected *(L—style)*. For example, in NaPVUS for one of the 1996 quarters, one of the people surveyed responded *(L—usage)*, as make and model for the vehicle selected, "Sable" and "Mercury," respectively *(L—syntax)*. The program that corrects the makes *(L—verbiage)* identified an error for "Sable," which is not found in the makes dictionary. The user, noticing the inversion of the make and model names, will therefore be able to correct this error.

The program will also indicate a problem for JEEP makes, which, naturally, is *(T—number)* not in the dictionary of automobile *(?)* makes. In this way, many errors were identified in the NaPVUS variable that indicate *(T—number, incorrect antecedent)* the type of vehicle selected to complete the fuel purchase diary. In fact *(T—mistranslation)*, this variable was used, at the beginning, to differentiate between cars and light trucks and vans to *(T—purpose function unclear)* form two files that are processed separately by the merge program. *(T—omission)* It turned out that, in some cases, a type of vehicle poorly specified *(L—syntax) (L—usage)* led to a truck being poorly *(T—mistranslation)* placed in the cars file, as illustrated in the preceding example, or vice versa. An adequately specified dictionary therefore *(T—shift)* allows certain information found in the study *(translation error repeated)* data to be authenticated (*syntax error repeated).* Finally *(T—shift)*, it is possible to identify make and model combinations that are erroneous (*L—verbiage*) with the two programs and the help of the dictionaries defined by the makes and models listed in the VFEES database. Such make and model combinations, which do *(T—tense)* not allow us *(?)* to properly identify the make and model of the vehicle, had to be eliminated from the merge process. ■

3. *TT argument schema/arrangement/organizational relations*
What is striking about this scientific/technical expository document is that, in spite of its length, there is little or no redundant information: the argument schema spans the whole text. Every procedure or variable explained is a part of the grounds for making the claim, so every element is part of the core argument. It follows that no section of the document can be considered of secondary importance in the context of TQA: every statement "counts."

For example, the translation "dictionary of automobile makes" for "dictionnaire des marques d'automobiles" at the beginning of the third paragraph may appear correct unless the full **co-text** is taken into account. Examination of the full text reveals that one of the key make subvariables for respondents' vehicles is the distinction between cars and light trucks/vans. The fact that the translator has not grasped this fundamental distinction is confirmed in the three subsequent sentences, which, in the ST, are designed to explain the purpose of the make correction program and the problems targeted. The translator adopts a word-for-word approach in the translation, as if to compensate for the failure to interpret in light of co-text, and the effects on propositional functions and the rendering of conjunctives and inference indicators are significant.

As explained above, a key element in the definition process does not come across clearly in the TT, and the rendering of the process-stage organizational relation is compromised as a result.

4. *Propositional functions/conjunctives/other inference indicators*
A functional analysis of the propositions in the three paragraphs reveals an intricate process of clarification and elaboration: after making a generalization as to the purpose of the preliminary processing and the correction programs, the writer explains each step or function (clarification) and then goes on to describe another feature of the procedure.

Thus in the third paragraph, the second and third sentences are clarifications of the initial statement (generalization) and the conjunctives *ainsi* and *en effet* are to be translated accordingly. The translator's actual renderings, *In this way* and *In fact,* fail to maintain fully and clearly the coherence of the ST. A clearer link between the first and second sentences would have been achieved by combining a conjunctive with lexical cohesion—that is, through repetition: "Thus the program identified many errors in the NaPVUS variable indicating the type of vehicle selected ..." The third sentence conveys another clarifying proposition, explaining the initial purpose of the variable (to differentiate cars from light trucks/vans), so the conjunctive *in fact,* with its function as qualification rather than clarification, is incorrect here. No conjunctive is required in the English. However, the conjunctive *Or,* opening the fourth sentence, is the sole exception to the clarification–elaboration development. Its function is clearly qualification, indicating that, in spite of the stated purpose of the variable, some vehicles were erroneously categorized. *However* should have been inserted to signpost the contrast.

The translation of the final two conjunctives in the paragraph, *donc* and *enfin,* raises questions too. The problem with the rendering *therefore* is that the reader automatically relates the consequence function to the immediately preceding sentence, from which the proposition "An adequately specified dictionary allows certain information found in the study data to be authenticated" cannot logically be derived. Cohesion by reference would have maintained the coherence here—for example, "An adequately specified dictionary allows information *of this kind...*" In the next sentence, *Finally* implies a sequence of steps, which is not the case within the paragraph as such. An additive such as *in addition* would have been correct here.

5. *Arguments*

On the surface, the text is a sequence of statistical and programming procedures accompanied by explanations of their content and purpose. In fact, the text can also be interpreted as a sequence of arguments based on the topic of *definition.* The purpose of the procedures is to ensure that the definition of a given variable in one survey database is matched as closely as possible by the definition of the same variable in the other database. The matching itself is achieved by *division,* a subtopic of definition. Thus the variable "make" is divided into cars and light trucks/vans and then subdivided into the makes themselves.

The variable is thus defined by its distinct components, which are themselves defined by means of the subtopic of *difference*: car vs. light truck/van, Mercury vs. Chevrolet.

Argument from definition is coupled with a second important argument from *relationship*, which underlies the error detection and correction process. Observations in the two databases are matched through the application of two relationship-based criteria: the pair of contraries *true/false* (Jeep = light truck/van vs. Jeep = car) and the pair of contradictions *existence/nonexistence* (information/missing information).

A third argument, used in the second paragraph, is from *comparison*, and specifically from *example*. The writer illustrates (*Par exemple, À titre d'illustration*) the types of problem solved by the correction program.

In the translation, the examples are rendered accurately, but the process of definition by division and relationship (or comparison) is obscured because the translator has not grasped the propositional functions of the text.

6. *Figures of speech*
The figure of personification is considered under "Narrative strategy."

7. *Narrative strategy*
This text contains few examples of first-person narration. On the contrary, "systems" are foregrounded, personified, and made subjects of the text. The correction program "inscrit/indicates," "corrige/corrects" and "offre une option/has an option." Thus the text is a prime illustration of Ouellet's premise that an impersonal "science" is writing the text. The translation conveys the personification adequately.

In addition, rather than using the narrator/statistician as agent or patient of the actions, the author resorts to impersonal forms and passivization without reference to any agent: for example, "modifications qui sont ajoutées," "toutes les entrées ... seront corrigées," "C'est ainsi qu'on a relevé plusieurs erreurs," "Il s'est avéré," and "dont il a été fait usage." While the translator renders such structures too literally, she avoids introducing the narrator except in the last sentence of the passage ("allow us"), so the scientific narrative style is by and large preserved. It is unlikely that this particular defect in the last sentence would have been counted as an error under the microtextual, quantitative model.

8. *Overall argumentation-centred TQA*

ARTRAQ Grid

Element	**Translation assessment**
Argument schema	Ground inaccurately rendered
Arrangement/ organizational relations	Inaccurately rendered
Propositional functions/ conjunctives/other inference Indicators	Inaccurately rendered
Arguments	Arguments from definition and relationship inaccurately rendered
Figures	N/A
Narrative strategy	Accurately rendered

Results of the analysis of the TT against a broad range of argumentation parameters reveal defects at several levels of argumentation. What is interesting here is that the failure to grasp and exploit the functions of the conjunctives exerts a multiplier effect, undermining interpretation of the grounds and individual arguments. While the ST passage pertains only to the grounds of the overall text, the grounds are part of the core argument. The TT is therefore inadequate.

Quantitative-microtextual TQA yields 10 minor translation errors and 7 minor language errors in the second and third paragraphs (400 words). Regarding the other two significant defects, the first (syntactic breakdown or incoherence) would be considered a grammatical peccadillo (plural for singular verb), and the second (*automobiles)* would be considered a minor translation error because the distinction between cars and trucks is mentioned later in the paragraph. Again, the evaluator's rating would have to be based on quantity alone.

The ARTRAQ model, on the other hand, brings out the weaknesses of the translation not as words, but as text, in the relationships between discourse components, thus demonstrating its inadequacy at several levels. First, the distinction between cars and light trucks/vans, which is central to the whole vehicle fuel efficiency measurement objective, is seriously compromised by the mistranslation of *automobiles;* the error would have been assessed as a major/critical one. Second, the argumentation of the grounds loses its cogency in the TT because the propositional development is undermined. As a result, the translation does not adequately reflect important elements of the grounds for the claim advanced toward the end of the document. The cumulative effect of propositional function/conjunctive errors may constitute a critical/major defect in itself.

The contradiction, or *contresens*, in *recognizes* (for *ne reconnaît pas*) in the first paragraph is outside the selected sample. In any case, rather than interpreting the switch from negative to positive microtextually, we can relate it to the propositional development of the passage as a whole. The function of the program is to identify and correct errors, as stated in the propositions preceding the one at issue. It "flags" deviations from terms in the predefined dictionary of makes, models, etc. In other words, it recognizes such items as not being part of the dictionary, so, in that sense, *recognizes* is at most a minor error.

Thus, in at least three instances, the ARTRAQ model produces a result of more probative or explanatory value than does the quantitative-microtextual approach and yields different judgments, sometimes more severe, sometimes more lenient.

Text 2

Title: *Recommandations sur les sources de données utilisées par le modèle TED, incluant des stratégies pour l'estimation de données manquantes / Recommendations on TEDM (Transportation Energy Demand Model) input data sources, including strategies for estimating missing data*

ST length: 11,000 words
Text type: report
Text mode: explanatory
Purpose: present the sources underlying a number of variables generated by the TEDM, an assessment of their statistical validity, and recommendations for modifications and additions to those sources
Text function: explanatory, but also argumentative because of evaluation and recommendation components
Translation purpose: same as ST

1. *Argument schema/arrangement/organizational relations*
Overall arrangement: Introduction–Recommendations–Conclusion–References–Appendixes.

In the "Recommendations" section, which accounts for 90% of the text, 22 variables are considered one by one. The analysis of each variable is a discrete component of the text, as was the explanation of each program function in text 1, and does not affect the analysis of other variables and related recommendations. Accordingly, in assessing TT quality, the evaluator will find no compensation, elsewhere in the text, for defects in the translation of a specific analysis of a variable.

The arrangement is conjunctive: sequential analysis of, and presentation of recommendations on, variables expressing energy efficiency in mathematical terms.

Argument Schema

Element	Description
Grounds	Strengths/weaknesses of data sources
Claim	Recommendations for modifications and additions
Warrant	Statistical methods and principles
Backing	Scientism (presupposed)
Qualifier	*Malheureusement* (bis), in commenting on weaknesses of certain sources
Rebuttal/restriction	N/A

Organizational relations: The relation is twofold: evidence–assertion (of strengths and weaknesses in a given source), and analysis/evaluation–recommendation.

2. *Reading of TT*

A cursory examination of the TT reveals no problems in the early sections but many target language weaknesses in the second half of the document: incorrect usage and lack of clarity.

Accordingly, the selected passages are taken from the second half of the document. They concern analysis of the variable "Commercial Use Estimated Average Annual per Truck Distance Travelled." Again, all sections of the ST contain parts of the core message.

Source text

(Para. 1) Deux types d'estimations, à considérer pour cette variable, de même que pour les variables estPerCarDist (Estimated Average Annual per Car Distance Travelled) et PUEstTrkDist (Personal Use Estimated Average Annual per Truck Distance Travelled), ont déjà été produites pour les besoins du modèle à partir de l'ENUVeP. D'abord, Victor Tremblay de STATPLUS a estimé, à la demande de l'OEE, la distance moyenne par véhicule selon différentes variables de segmentation sous-jacentes au modèle TED, telles que le type d'utilisation (privé versus commercial) et l'âge des véhicules. En raison d'un nombre non négligeable de véhicules non conduits durant la période d'enquête, l'approche retenue par STATPLUS consistait à estimer, dans un premier temps, la probabilité qu'un véhicule soit utilisé, puis à estimer ensuite la distance parcourue en fonction de son utilisation. Plus précisément, la méthode consistait à multiplier la probabilité qu'un véhicule d'une catégorie donnée soit utilisé par la distance moyenne parcourue par les véhicules de cette catégorie, lorsque ces véhicules sont effectivement utilisés (voir Tremblay (2000) pour la méthodologie détaillée). À notre avis, une approche de type tobit ou une procédure d'Heckman en deux étapes (à titre d'approximation pour le tobit) aurait dû être privilégiée pour la production de ces estimations.

(Para. 2) Rappelons également le travail de modélisation fait par le Compendium lors du projet sur les séries de données nationales à compléter, qui a été réalisé dans le cadre du plan de travail de l'an passé (voir Boucher et Bonin, mai 2000). Ce projet a permis de combler le vide entre l'ECC et l'ENUVeP et d'obtenir, entre autres, des séries complètes sur la distance annuelle parcourue en moyenne par une voiture de 1980 à 1996 et par un camion léger de 1982 à 1996.

...

■ (Para. 3) L'intérêt du précédent projet est qu'il fournit des estimations de la distance parcourue qui fluctuent au fil des années au lieu de considérer les valeurs constantes, comme cela semble être le cas présentement dans le modèle. Par contre, les données ne sont pas disponibles en fonction de l'âge exact des véhicules, mais plutôt suivant quatre groupes d'âge : 2 ans et moins, 3-5 ans, 6-8 ans, 9 ans et plus. La possibilité de produire, à l'aide des outils d'analyse bayesienne développés par Mme Nathalie Boucher, des séries équivalentes à l'échelle provinciale ou régionale (Maritimes,

Québec, Ontario, Prairies, Colombie-Britannique) devrait être étudiée lors d'une prochaine entente.

(Para. 4) Dans sa révision de l'inventaire des variables d'entrée, l'OEE a indiqué que le CVS (1999-) pourrait constituer une nouvelle source de données pour cette variable. Cette enquête se veut en effet une source précieuse de données pour l'estimation de la distance parcourue. Notons que l'enquête a une couverture plus large que celle requise par la présente variable et qu'elle se veut, en conséquence, également une source d'intérêt pour la variable estHTrkPVDT (Estimated Heavy Truck per Vehicle Distance Travelled). L'enquête CVS a été conçue pour l'estimation des distances parcourues par les diverses catégories de véhicules routiers, dont les camions légers, moyens et lourds. Dans le carnet de déplacements destiné aux véhicules légers (voitures et camions), on demande au répondant de préciser le motif d'utilisation du véhicule pour chacun des déplacements (question 7 de la version 2000) et un des motifs de la liste est l'utilisation pour le travail (« Driving as part of the job »). Les estimations de distance pour les camions légers peuvent donc être segmentées suivant le type d'usage (privé ou commercial), permettant de cibler spécifiquement la distance commerciale pour les fins de la présente variable. Le carnet pour les camions de masse supérieure (moyens et lourds), dont l'usage est par défaut commercial, recueille également la distance parcourue par chacun des véhicules sélectionnés pour chacun de leurs déplacements, lors de la période à l'étude. Les deux catégories de poids des véhicules retenues pour la stratification de l'échantillon, 10 000-33 000 lbs et plus de 33 000 lbs, permettent ensuite de produire des estimations séparées pour les camions moyens (présente variable) et les camions lourds (variable estHTrkPVDT). Une estimation de la distance commerciale totale de chacune des deux catégories de camions peut ainsi être obtenue. ■ La procédure d'estimation de la distance annuelle moyenne consiste simplement à prendre une moyenne pondérée des distances hebdomadaires (distance cumulée sur les sept jours d'enquête) associées aux déplacements d'une catégorie donnée, puis à extrapoler à l'année les résultats hebdomadaires obtenus. La pondération adéquate des résultats pour l'obtention de résultats annuels sera dictée par Statistique Canada, sur la base des poids statistiques calculés par l'organisme.

(Para. 5) Soulignons que les données de l'enquête permettent de répondre aux besoins de segmentation de cette variable, à savoir, la désagrégation possible selon la province, la taille du camion et le type de carburant consommé. La province apparaissant dans le fichier du CVS correspond à la province d'immatriculation du véhicule et non à la province où il est effectivement utilisé. Notons que si on s'intéresse à la distance parcourue sur les routes d'une province donnée pour les camions moyens et lourds, seul le carnet d'enquête de 1999 sera utile à cet égard puisque l'on demandait au répondant de fournir l'origine et la destination précise de chaque déplacement (ville et province). L'instrument d'enquête a toutefois été modifié depuis et le carnet de 2000 ne permet plus de recueillir ces informations. Désormais, on demande seulement au chauffeur du camion de spécifier si le déplacement s'est fait à l'intérieur d'une même province, s'il s'agit d'un déplacement interprovincial ou si la frontière Canada/États-Unis a été traversée. Quant à la segmentation par âge du véhicule, il faudra probablement refaire le lien entre les données du CVS et celles des fichiers d'immatriculation ayant servi lors de l'échantillonnage si l'on veut retrouver l'année de fabrication du véhicule.

Target text

(Para. 1) Two types of estimates, to consider for this variable, *(L—punctuation)* as well as for the variables estPerCarDist (Estimated Average Annual per Car Distance Travelled) and PUEstTrkDist (Personal Use Estimated Average Annual per Truck Distance Travelled), have already been produced for model requirements from NaPVUS. First, Victor Tremblay from STATPLUS estimated, at the request of the OEE, the average distance per vehicle according to different variables of segmentation underlying the TEDM, such as the type of use (personal versus commercial) and the age of the vehicles. Because a good number of the vehicles were not driven during the survey period, the approach retained *(L—gallicism)* by STATPLUS consisted in estimating, first, *(T—repetition of temporal conjunctive makes sequence of propositions unclear)* the probability of a vehicle being used, then to estimate its distance travelled conditionally to its use *(L—usage)*. More precisely, it consisted in multiplying the probability that a vehicle from a given category be *(L—verb form)* used for *(**X** major T—mistranslation)* the average distance travelled by vehicles of this category, when these vehicles are effectively used (see Tremblay (2000) for detailed methodology). In our opinion, a tobit type approach or a Heckman process in two stages (as an approximation for the tobit) should have been used for producing the estimates.

(Para. 2) We also recall *(T—mistranslation)* that modelling work was done by the Compendium for the project on the national data series to complete what was done for *(**Y** major T—mistranslation)* the work plan last year (see Boucher and Bonin, May 2000). This project made it possible to fill the gap between FCS and NaPVUS and obtain, among others *(L—gallicism)*, complete series of *(L—prepositional usage)* annual distance travelled on average by a car from 1980 to 1996 and by a light truck from 1982 to 1996.

...

■ (Para. 3) The advantage of the previous *(T—mistranslation)* project is that it provides estimates for the distance travelled that fluctuate with the years instead of being considered constant values, as it *(L—usage)* seems to be the case currently with this model. However, the data is not available according to the exact age of the vehicles, but rather according to age groups: 2 years and under, 3-5 years, 6-8 years, 9 years and over. The possibility, by using Bayesian analysis tools developed by Ms Nathalie Boucher, *(L—syntax)* of producing series equivalent to *(**Z** major T—mistranslation)* the provincial or regional scale (Maritimes, Quebec, Ontario, Prairies, British Columbia) should be studied for the next agreement.

(Para. 4) In its review of input variables, the OEE indicates that the CVS (1999-) could constitute a new source of data for this variable. The survey is supposed, in effect *(T—mistranslation)*, to be an important source of data for estimating distance travelled. We *(T—mistranslation)* note that the survey covers more than the requirements *(T—mistranslation)* for the present variable and consequently is also assumed to be a good source for the variable estHTrkPVDT (Estimated Heavy Truck per Vehicle Distance Travelled). The CVS survey was designed to estimate distances travelled by *(T—omission)* various categories of road vehicles, including light, medium and heavy trucks. In the travel log book for light vehicles (cars and trucks), we *(T—mistranslation)* asked our *(error repeated)* respondent to specify vehicle use for each trip (question 7 of the 2000 version) and one of the uses on the list refers to work use ("Driving as part of the job"). Distance estimates for light trucks can therefore be segmented according to the type of use (personal or commercial), making it possible to specifically *(L—redundant)* target commercial distance for the purposes of the present *(L—usage)* variable. The log book for higher mass

(L—terminology) trucks (medium and heavy), used by default for commercial purposes, also shows the distance travelled for each of the vehicles selected for each of their trips, during the survey period. The two weight categories of the vehicles retained *(L—gallicism)* for sample stratification, 10 000-33 000 lbs and over 33 000 lbs, then make it possible to produce separate estimates for medium trucks (present variable) and heavy trucks (variable estHTrkPVDT). An estimate of the total commercial distance for each of the two categories of trucks can thus be obtained. *(L—article omitted)* ■ Estimation procedure for the average annual distance consists in simply taking a weighted average of weekly distances (cumulated *(L—terminology)* distance over seven days of survey) corresponding to the trips of a given category, then extrapolate *(L—grammar)* the weekly results obtained for *(T—ambiguity)* the year. Appropriate weighting of the results to obtain annual results will be provided by Statistics Canada, on the basis of statistical weight *(T—number)* calculated by them.

(Para. 5) The survey data enables us to meet the segmentation requirements of this variable, i.e. disaggregation possible according to province, truck size and type of fuel used. The province appearing in the CVS file corresponds to the province where the vehicle is registered and not the province where it is in fact used. Note that if we want to consider the distance travelled on roads of a specific province by medium and heavy trucks, only the 1999 survey log book will be useful in this respect since we *(T—error repeated)* asked the respondent to provide precise origin and destination of each trip (city and province). The survey instrument, however, has been changed since and the 2000 log book does not give us this information. Now, we *(error repeated)* only ask the driver of the truck to specify whether the trip will be *(T—tense)* within the same province, interprovincial or a border crossing into the United States *(L—no parallel structure)*. With regard to segmentation by vehicle age, there would *(T—tense)* probably have to be *(L—syntax)* a connection re-established between CVS data and registration files that were used during sampling in order to find the year the vehicle was manufactured.

3. *TT argument schema/arrangement/organizational relations*

As in text 1, the argument schema spans the whole text. Evidence of strengths and weaknesses in various data sources (grounds) and the recommendations (claims) predicated on those grounds are present in each analysis of a variable. We can therefore make the assumption that few, if any, propositions are of secondary importance in the context of TQA.

Examining the above ST passage, we find the following argument schema elements:

Element	**Description**
Ground 1	Use of American sources to calculate this variable
Claim 1	Canadian sources should be used where possible
Ground 2	Strengths of Canadian sources: NaPVUS, Boucher & Bonin study
Claim 2	These specific Canadian sources should be integrated in the TEDM
Warrant	Statistical methods and principles
Backing	Scientism
Qualifier	Paragraph 3: "comme cela semble être le cas présentement ..."
Rebuttal/restriction	Weaknesses of specific Canadian sources

Does the translation render these elements adequately? The translation contains three conventionally and intrinsically serious defects: items ***X*** (para. 1), ***Y*** (para. 2), and ***Z*** (para. 3). Translation ***X*** is incoherent, since the second component of the multiplication operation is not clearly identified; in ***Y***, the relationship of the modelling project to the work plan is misconstrued; and in ***Z***, *à l'échelle* is mistranslated and the type of series is not clearly characterized. Do these mistranslations jeopardize the reader's understanding of the propositions sufficiently for the core argument to be misunderstood? In ***Y***, the error does not diminish the reader's understanding of the purpose or content of the project concerned; they are outlined in subsequent sentences. The other two mistranslations bear on a criticism of a potential data source (***X***) and on the potential of another method (***Z***), and as such, they directly affect a ground, a warrant, and a claim conveyed in the ST. Note, however, that only ***Z*** is part of the sample selected for quantitative TQA purposes.

Organizational relations: The serious defects compromise the force of the "evidence" component of the evidence–assertion relation.

4. *Propositional functions/conjunctives/other inference indicators*
A functional analysis of the propositions in paragraph 4 reveals the following general structure in each paragraph:

1. **Generalization**—a statement in the form of a recommendation on data sources or a specific data source
2. **Clarification**—justification of the recommendation by explaining the purpose and content of the source, introduced by the conjunctive *en effet*
3. **Elaboration** of the clarification
4. **Consequence**—potential of the resulting estimates and calculations (*en conséquence*)
5. **Elaboration**—purpose of CVS survey
6. **Consequence**—segmentation potential (*donc)*
7. **Elaboration** (*également)*
8. **Elaboration** (*ensuite)*
9. **Consequence** (*ainsi)*
10. **Clarification** (*consiste simplement ... puis)*
11. **Clarification** (*La pondération adéquate)*

The translation reflects this process adequately except in proposition 2, where *in effect* does not render the function of *en effet* as an introduction to a justification.

5. *Arguments*
Two topics are at play here: *testimony*, in the form of *statistical* evidence, and *comparison*, in the form of evaluation of the *degree* to which those statistics can be combined to generate general efficiency-related estimates. The closer the data concerned approach completeness or, in terms of argumentation, the closer the part approaches the whole, the more suitable the data source is. Apart from mistranslation ***X*** (outside the sample), the evaluative arguments are adequately rendered.

6. *Figures*
N/A.

7. *Narrative strategy*
Narrative strategy is central to the overall argumentation strategy in this text. The first-person-plural pronoun and verb form occurs in ST

at the metadiscourse level: *Rappelons, Soulignons,* etc. Elsewhere the author adheres scrupulously to the impersonal forms of scientific discourse. The translator does not recognize the first-person feature of French discourse for what it is—a linking or introductory device—and translates the first as "We also recall." More interesting, however, is the fact that, in this and other passages, the "presence" of the first-person narrator is extended to the translation of the impersonal pronoun "on." In paragraphs 4 and 5, for example, the narrator introduces questions in two separate surveys with the words "on demande"—"the respondent is asked." By translating *on* as *we,* the translator unwittingly makes the author-evaluator the author of the surveys being evaluated: "We note that the [CVS] survey covers more than the requirements for the present variable ... we asked our respondent to specify vehicle use. ... " There are two possible interpretative consequences: either the reader finds the narrative scheme incoherent or he or she loses confidence in the objectivity, and therefore the credibility, of the author. In both cases, but particularly in the second, the force of the grounds and claims is adversely affected in the TT.

8. *Overall argumentation-centred TQA*

ARTRAQ Grid

Element	**Translation assessment**
Argument schema	Grounds, warrant, and rebuttal/restriction inaccurately rendered
Arrangement/ organizational relations	Inaccurately rendered
Propositional functions/ conjunctives/other inference indicators	Inaccurately rendered
Arguments	Accurately rendered
Figures	N/A
Narrative strategy	Inaccurately rendered

Results of the analysis of the TT against a broad range of argumentation parameters show that while many items (propositional functions, conjunctives, arguments) are accurately rendered, significant items relating to the content of certain grounds and claims were misconstrued and the erroneous attribution of authorial responsibility increases the potential for misinterpretation on the reader's part.

Quantitative-microtextual TQA of the selected sample (paragraphs 3 and 4) yields 1 major translation error, 6 minor translation errors, and 7 minor language errors.

By reading the TT, without reference to the ST, the evaluator can determine the nature of the grounds and claims in the text and, in the case of the first and third "significant" defects, identify problems with certain elements of the argument schema. Comparison with the corresponding ST elements confirms that grounds and claims have been seriously affected in the TT. In the quantitative TQA, it is questionable whether any of the three "significant" defects would have been characterized as major errors, since no core argument structure has been established as a reference point for assessing the "centrality" of the defects concerned.

Similarly, the erroneous shift in narrative voice from *on* to *we* would not be considered important without reference to the concept of narrative strategy, and the translator's lack of familiarity with features of scientific discourse might well not be considered a significant shortcoming.

5.2.2 *Criminal justice and criminology translations*

The texts under consideration here were translated for publication in the Canadian Criminal Justice Association's periodical *Justice Today/ Actualités-Justice*. In each case, the author focuses on the adverse impact of social and cultural trends and perceptions on the criminal justice system. Each text is overtly argumentative, and we may therefore assume that the features of argumentation and rhetoric outlined in the chapters on methodology will be exploited more intensively than in the statistics texts. The translations were submitted by freelancers as drafts for revision prior to delivery to the client.

Text 3

ST length: 1668 words
Text type: article for professional association periodical
Text mode: argumentative
Purpose: persuade reader that responsibility for criminal acts belongs

not only to the perpetrators but also to the rich and powerful, who create the conditions under which crime becomes attractive and necessary

SOURCE TEXT

LE CRIME AURAIT-IL DES SOUBASSEMENTS?

Est-il vrai, comme on l'a déjà prétendu et comme certains le croient encore, que chaque société a les crimes et les criminels qu'elle mérite? Que chaque contexte suscite ses crimes et ses criminels bien à lui? Que tel système économique débouche sur des crimes que n'engendre pas ou engendre moins une autre relation avec l'argent? Que telle culture se dispense allègrement de l'emprisonnement sans s'en porter plus mal? Durkheim, en tout cas, qui n'était pas le dernier venu, pensait que chaque société avait « son » taux de suicide.

Soulever de telles questions, ce n'est pas, que je sache, évacuer la responsabilité personnelle ni excuser par un quelconque déterminisme le crime que commet l'individu X ce soir à minuit. Je penserais plutôt le contraire. En effet, croire que la criminalité est en partie imputable à l'organisation sociale, loin de gommer la responsabilité des individus, a plutôt comme conséquence d'élargir le cercle des personnes dont la responsabilité est engagée dans la criminalité. Car, dans cette perspective, la responsabilité se partage entre ceux qui commettent le crime et ceux qui créent les conditions propices au crime, entre ceux que pourchasse la police et que sanctionnent les tribunaux et ceux qui, sans avoir l'air d'y toucher et sans même encourir de reproches, rendent le crime plus séduisant ou plus probable.

Ne jamais poser de questions à la seconde catégorie de personnes, c'est concentrer l'attention sur le résultat, rarement sur les incitations, jamais sur les causes. Tel était peut-être le raisonnement (moqueur) que se faisait Mark Twain quand il demandait ceci : « Un homme vole une banque. Qui faut-il punir : l'homme qui a volé la banque ou l'homme qui a créé la banque... ? »

Lâcheté et hypocrisie

Premier exemple des comportements qui favorisent discrètement l'expansion du crime : la perpétuation des hypocrisies. Ou, si l'on préfère un langage plus feutré, la distance imprudemment maintenue entre un puritanisme idéologique et les comportements quotidiens des humains. Une loi trop sévère ou trop éloignée du consensus social ressemblera toujours à ce qu'on disait autrefois de l'obéissance jésuite : « Une tyrannie absolue tempérée par le mauvais vouloir des sujets ».

Malgré cette vérité cent fois corroborée, beaucoup de nos gouvernants parient toujours que la tyrannie du texte l'emportera sur les vouloirs bons ou mauvais des sujets. C'est une erreur dont le crime a vite fait de profiter : la distance artificiellement maintenue entre la loi et le comportement des gens fournit de rentables créneaux aux pires fripouilles. Malgré l'exemple de la prohibition américaine que la mafia a si bien (?) exploitée, notre société maintient toujours des interdictions dont nous voyons quotidiennement la futilité et, pire encore, les effets désastreux. Dans le cas d'une bonne partie des drogues douces, on devrait savoir, au moins depuis le rapport Le Dain, que les préjugés sont presque la seule base de l'interdiction. Dans le cas des toxicomanies plus lourdes, c'est à une forme ou à une autre de légalisation contrôlée qu'une société réaliste avait recours. L'interdiction est, en effet, coûteuse, inapplicable, propice au développement des empires criminels. En s'arc-boutant sur les interdictions actuelles, nos législateurs se comportent, comme aurait dit un marxiste de stricte allégeance, en alliés objectifs du crime organisé.

Justice et argent

Une deuxième façon discrète et impunie de contribuer au crime, c'est de faire semblant que la pauvreté et l'aisance n'ont aucune importance dans l'évolution de la criminalité ni d'ailleurs dans le fonctionnement de la justice. Pourtant, juger et sanctionner le crime sans tenir compte de la situation économique des individus et de la société, c'est verser dans la myopie et dans l'injustice. Tel est pourtant le comportement de ceux qui réduisent d'année en année le financement de l'aide juridique, qui continuent à jeter dans les plateaux d'une même balance la liberté et l'argent, qui refusent de formuler les peines pécuniaires en termes de « revenus quotidiens », qui définissent les peines minima sans faire entrer la situation économique de l'accusé en ligne de compte.

Qu'on se rassure : je ne suis pas en train d'affirmer que la pauvreté justifie le crime ni que les pauvres sont les auteurs de la plupart des crimes. Je dis tout simplement qu'une société dont les citoyens s'appauvrissent est une société que l'anarchie, le désordre et le crime menacent de plus près. Une telle société ne peut empêcher le travail au noir, l'exploitation souterraine des plus vulnérables, les types les plus répugnants de corruption. Si l'on admet cela, des questions méritent de remonter jusqu'à ceux qui, par paresse, par calcul politique ou par simple sottise, plongent les gens dans le désespoir ou empêchent les plus pauvres d'obtenir justice.

Car le fait est là, même si les Don Quichotte impénitents sont les seuls à le rappeler : celui qui met à pied des centaines ou des milliers de personnes ne prend pas une décision purement économique. Il contribue aussi, qu'il en soit conscient ou non, à l'appauvrissement des plus pauvres et à la multiplication des raccourcis plus ou moins grisâtres qui leur sont alors offerts. Dans une société cassée en deux, toute décision qui influe sur l'emploi range son auteur dans l'un des deux camps, celui du marteau ou celui de l'enclume. Qu'il soit permis de vérifier si celui qui manie le marteau sait sur quoi et sur qui il frappe.

Si notre marteleur affirme, le front haut, que la mondialisation exige des coupes claires dans l'emploi, il faut lui demander s'il a internalisé les coûts de son geste, si, en d'autres termes, il a évalué ce que ses « rationalisations » coûtent à la société, non seulement en soutiens sociaux, mais aussi en lutte contre la criminalité. Car la gestion n'est pas un VTT qui circule dans le désert. Mondialiser sans mesurer la portée qu'ont les décisions au-delà de la bulle des dirigeants d'entreprise, ce n'est certes pas faire tomber les frontières ni s'ouvrir au monde extérieur. Le pire travail au noir qu'on puisse imaginer, c'est, en effet, celui de l'entreprise qui gonfle ses dividendes à coups de mises à pied et qui refile à l'État le coût du chômage qu'elle a causé. À moi le bénéfice, à d'autres les charges sociales. Quand, corollaire prévisible des « rationalisations », le chômage pousse à l'affolement, à la pauvreté, voire à la délinquance, le principe de l'internalisation des coûts exige l'examen de toutes les responsabilités, y compris celles de la gestion. Malheureusement, nous n'en sommes pas (encore) à cette idée de l'internalisation. Le chômage planifié ne fait donc pas partie de ce que le Code criminel appellerait l'incitation au crime.

Encore et toujours l'argent

■ (Para. 1) L'appauvrissement, que les dirigeants d'entreprise semblent considérer comme un « acte du Ciel » même si ce sont eux qui brandissent la foudre divine, modifie beaucoup de comportements individuels et sociaux. Il incite à la sauvagerie, mais, en plus, il rend impossible le recours aux moyens de défense usuels dans une société civilisée. Comment celui qui crève de faim pourrait-il résister à la tentation de se faire justice quand la justice est hors de prix? Songeons, à cet égard, à certaines explosions récentes d'insatisfaction populaire : ne peut-on pas y voir, outre une érosion de la société de droit, un jugement sévère sur l'efficacité et les coûts de la justice traditionnelle?

(Para. 2) On constate aujourd'hui, par exemple, car il s'agit d'une évidence admise même par divers ministres provinciaux, que la justice ne fait plus partie des droits que peut exercer le citoyen moyen. On le voit, on le sait, on le déplore, on s'y résigne, mais nul Barreau ne semble vraiment préoccupé par une justice de moins en moins accessible. La charte constitutive de l'ordre professionnel des plaideurs a beau lui imposer comme première fonction l'intérêt public, le fait qu'une majorité de citoyens ne peut plus se payer un avocat ne change pas la mentalité de l'ordre. Or, c'est patent : l'accusé nanti peut payer un procureur, mais pas le citoyen moyen. Le citoyen privilégié peut défendre ses droits, faire valoir son innocence présumée, négocier une peine allégée, mais pas le pauvre ni, moins encore, le citoyen de la classe moyenne.

(Para. 3) On voit se resserrer l'étau. D'un côté de ses crocs, l'appauvrissement renforce l'attrait des raccourcis criminels. De l'autre, l'appauvrissement expose les délinquants moins argentés à des peines plus lourdes. Quand ces mâchoires se rapprochent, a-t-on le droit de rappeler à ceux qui les commandent que les dirigeants d'entreprise mondialisent surtout la misère et l'injustice s'ils passent le chômage par pertes et profits?

A-t-on appris?

(Para. 4) Le crime dont on parle et dont on s'occupe, est-ce toujours, comme au temps de Dickens ou de Hugo, celui que commet l'affamé, l'affolé, le petit truand? La responsabilité du crime peut-elle, au contraire, reposer de temps à autre sur les épaules des décideurs qui privent les démunis de leurs droits et de leur sécurité et qui propulsent un nombre croissant de citoyens en marge de la société?

(Para. 5) Que seuls les riches ou les assistés sociaux puissent en principe obtenir la défense pleine et entière de leurs droits, voilà une sinistre réalité que l'on ne dénonce pas et que les juristes ne voient peut-être même plus. ■ Que, de plus en plus, les citoyens aient à tolérer l'intolérable, qu'ils doivent laisser les bandes de motards criminalisés intimider les petits fermiers jusqu'à l'esclavage, voilà qui n'émeut personne. Celui que salit un démagogue au micro d'une tribune téléphonique ne pourra triompher de l'artillerie juridique des réseaux radiophoniques que s'il est riche et obstiné.

L'actualité abonde en questions fondamentales; nous sommes, malheureusement, suréquipés en astuces pour les esquiver. À croire que l'instruction, au lieu de transmettre le savoir en même temps que le sens des responsabilités, ancre plutôt dans l'esquive, dans le ponce-pilatisme, dans le va-voir-ailleurs. À croire que la multiplication des diplômes, à défaut de favoriser ouvertement les disparités sociales, ne vise même plus à les réduire. Puisqu'on parvient toujours à opposer un sophisme à chacun des drames sociaux, preuve est faite que ces drames achèvent de passer à la trappe. Donc, tout va bien. Se pourrait-il, quand même, que le crime ait établi certaines de ses assises dans de fort beaux domaines?

TARGET TEXT

IS CRIME BUILT ON SOLID FOUNDATIONS?

Is there some truth to the old adage, that *(L—grammar, pronoun usage)* some people still believe, that each society has the crimes and criminals that it deserves? That each set of circumstances produces its own crimes and criminals? That a given economic system results in crimes that either do not exist or occur less frequently in others? *(Major T—mistranslation)* That a given culture can blithely forgo handing out prison sentences without being any the worse for it? In any case, Durkheim, who knew something about the subject, believed that each society has its "own" suicide rate.

Raising such questions does not, that *(L—grammar)* I am aware, eliminate personal responsibility or, using any *(T—mistranslation)* brand of determinism, absolve John Doe of the crime he will commit at midnight tonight. I would tend to think just the opposite. Indeed, thinking that crime is partly attributable to social structure, rather than relieving individuals of their responsibility, increases the circle of people responsible for crime. Looking at the issue from this perspective, responsability *(L—misspelling)* is shared between those who commit crimes as well as those who create the conditions giving rise to them, between those chased by the police and punished by the courts, *(L—punctuation)* and those who, without seeming to have anything to do with the situation and are *(T—mistranslation)* even above reproach, make crime more appealing and even more probable.

Never questioning this second category of people focuses *(T—omission)* mainly on the results of crime, rarely on what makes it more attractive and never on its causes. Perhaps that was Mark Twain's (cynical) reasoning when he asked who should be punished when a man robs a bank? *(L—indirect question)* The one who robbed the bank or the one who owns it?

Cowardice and Hypocrisy

Let us look at the perpetuation of hypocrisy as our first example of behaviour that discreetly favours *(T—mistranslation)* increasing crime. Or, if you prefer milder language, the unwisely maintained gap between ideological puritanism and everyday human behaviour *(L—verb omitted)*. Law that is too severe or a *(T—omission)* long way from social consensus will always bring to mind what used to be said of Jesuit obedience: "Absolute authority tempered by the bad will of the people."

In spite of this truth having been corroborated over and over again, many of our leaders still expect that the sovereignty *(T—mistranslation)* of an enactment *(T—mistranslation)* will triumph over the will, be it good or bad, of the people. Crime has been quick to take advantage of this error: the artificially maintained distance between the law and people's behaviour provides profitable markets for the worst crooks. In spite of the example of American Prohibition, which the Mafia exploited so well, our society still insists on certain interdictions whose obvious futility and *(L—comma required)* worse yet, disastrous effects can be seen on a daily basis. It should be obvious to everyone—at least since the Le Dain Report was released—that prejudices are practically the only reason for making *(T—omission)* soft drugs illegal. For other, harder drugs, a realistic society would turn to some form or another of controlled legalization. Indeed, making certain substances illegal is expensive, unenforceable and favours *(T—gallicism)* the development of criminal empires. By supporting these interdictions *(L—gallicism)*, our lawmakers are behaving, as card-carrying Marxists would say, like impartial allies of organized crime.

Money and Justice

A second unobstrusive *(L—typo)* and unpunishable *(T—shift)* way of contributing to crime is pretending that being rich or poor is not an important factor in the evolution *(T—mistranslation)* of criminality *(L—gallicism)* or in the functionning *(L—typo)* of justice. However, judging and punishing crime without taking into account the economic circumstances of individuals and society is shortsighted and injust *(L—misspelling)*. However, this is exactly how those who continue to cut, year after year, funding for legal aid, or continue to put money and liberty on the same side of the scale (*T—mistranslation*), or refuse to set fines in accordance with "daily income" or define minimum penalties without taking into account the economic circumstances of the accused behave.

Do not think *(T—mistranslation)* that I am trying *(T—mistranslation)* to state that poverty justifies crime or that the poor commit most crimes. I am simply saying that a society whose citizens are becoming poorer is a society more strongly threatened by anarchy, disorder and crime. Such a society cannot prevent people from working under the table, illegally *(T—mistranslation)* exploiting the most vulnerable or resorting to the most reprehensible types of corruption. If we admit this, some questions deserve to be asked of those who, through laziness, political calculation or simple stupidity, allow people to sink into despair or prevent the poorest from obtaining justice.

Because the fact remains *(L—verb omitted)* that employers who lay off hundreds or thousands of workers are not making purely economic decisions, even if only the unabashed Don Quixotes *(L—incomplete idiom)* recognize it. These employers are also contributing, consciously or not, to the impoverishment of the poorest and to the proliferation of the generally *(T—mistranslation)* shady corner cutting made possible by their decisions *(T—mistranslation)*. In a divided society, every decision that impacts on employment puts its maker in one of two camps: hammer or anvil. Let us make sure that those who wield the hammer know who *(L—grammar)* and what they are hitting.

If our hammer wielders state, heads held high, that globalization demands significant job cuts, we must ask them if they have internalized the costs of their actions, or, in other words, if they have calculated what their "rationalizations" will cost society, not only for social assistance, but also for fighting crime. Because management does not operate in a vacuum. Globalization *(L—part of speech)* without taking into account its effects beyond the corporate bubble will certainly not break down any borders or lead to an opening up to the outside world. Indeed, the case where a business maximizes its dividends by laying off its workers and passing on the cost of the resulting unemployment to the State is the worst sort of working under the table imaginable. "I'll take the profits; you can have the social costs." When, as a predictable consequence of these "rationalizations", unemployment leads to panic, poverty, and even crime, the principle of cost internalization demands all responsible factors be examined *(L—usage)*, including management. Unfortunately, we have not (yet) reached this concept *(T—shift)* of internalization. Thus, planned unemployment does not constitute what the criminal code *(L—lower case)* would call abetting crime.

The Role of Money

■ (Para. 1) Impoverishment, which management seems to consider an "Act *(L—upper case)* of God" even though management is the one in control, greatly impacts on individual and social behaviour. In addition to leading to unsocial behaviour, it renders recourse to usual means of defence in a civilized society impossible. How can those who are starving resist the temptation to make their own justice when traditional justice is beyond their reach? Bearing this in mind *(T—mistranslation)*, let us think about several recent eruptions of popular dissatisfaction. Can we not see, other than *(T—shift)* the erosion of a just *(T—mistranslation)* society, a harsh judgment on the effectiveness and costs of traditional justice?

(Para. 2) For example, it is obvious (even several provincial ministers admit it) that, in this day and age, average citizens no longer have the means to exercise their rights to justice. We can see it, be aware of it, *(L—space)* deplore it and resign ourselves to it, but no Bar seems to be really concerned by the decreasing accessibility to *(L—prepositional usage)* justice. The constitution of the professional order of lawyers may have tried *(T—mistranslation)* to make the interests of the public *(L—terminology)* its first priority, but the fact that the majority of citizens cannot afford to pay a lawyer is not changing the mentality of the order. However *(T—illogical link word)*, it is obvious that a well-off person accused of a crime can pay a lawyer, but not the average citizen. Privileged citizens can defend their rights, prove *(T—mistranslation)* their presumed innocence and negotiate lighter sentences; *(L—punctuation)* whereas, the poor, and even less *(T—mistranslation)*, the middle-class citizen cannot.

(Para. 3) We can see the door closing. On one hand, poverty makes criminal behaviour more attractive. On the other, poorer criminals receive harsher sentences. When the door does slam shut, do we have the right to remind those in charge that management is, above all *(T—shift because of word order)*, globalizing poverty and injustice if profits and losses are more important than unemployment? *(T—mistranslation)*

Have We Learned?

(Para. 4) Are we talking and concerning ourselves about the type of crime committed by those who are starving, terrified or petty thieves, as in the time of Dickens and Hugo? Or, conversely, does the responsibility for crime sometimes rest squarely on the shoulders of the decision makers who deprive the impoverished of their rights and security and marginalize a growing number of citizens?

(Para. 5) The fact that only the rich or those on social assistance are able, in theory, to get a full and fair defense *(L—U.S. spelling)* of their rights is an ominous reality *(L—redundant)* that society does not denounce and lawyers maybe no longer even see. ■ The fact that citizens have to increasingly tolerate the intolerable, allow criminal motorcycle gangs to intimidate samll *(L—typo)* farmers to the point of slavery no longer moves anyone. Individuals slandered by demagogues on open-line broadcasts *(T—mistranslation)* can only triumph over the legal artillery of the radio networks if they are rich and perseverant *(L—neologism)*.

Current events teem with fundamental questions, which, unfortunately, we are very adept at sidestepping. It seems that education, rather than imparting knowledge and a sense of responsibility, results in evasion, washing our hands of unpalatable situations and passing the buck *(L—lack of parallelism)*. It seems that the increasing number of degrees granted, *(L—comma splice)* does not even reduce social disparities *(T—omission)*; in fact it actually *(T—mistranslation)* seeems *(L—typo)* to favour *(T—mistranslation)* them. The fact that we always manage to come up with an equivocation *(T—mistranslation)* for each social tragedy is proof that we end up sweeping them under the carpet. Therefore *(T—mistranslation)*, everything is fine. However, could it be that crime has managed to penetrate some very high circles? *(T—mistranslation)*

TEXT 3 ASSESSMENT

1. Argument schema/arrangement/organizational relations

Arrangement

1. **Introduction**: *corrective* in type, presenting the thesis that, contrary to popular opinion, responsibility for crime belongs not only to those who commit it but also to those who create the conditions for it.
2. **Argument 1**: tougher laws actually foster crime, e.g., American Prohibition, banning certain drugs. Such laws are hypocritical since they are based on prejudice.
3. **Argument 2**: money influences crime and justice.
    - Unjust to mete out punishment without regard for economic circumstances of individuals and society
    - Responsibility of those who, by cutting funding for legal aid, cause despair
    - Danger of globalization without considering human cost: responsibility of employers who generate profits by laying off workers and transferring costs to society
    - Poverty leads to crime
    - Only the rich and, to a lesser extent, those on social assistance can obtain full defence of their rights in court
    - Lawyers no longer give priority to protecting the public interest
4. **Conclusion**:
    - Society must increasingly tolerate the intolerable because the average person cannot afford to take legal action and the legal professionals do not seem to care
    - Education has not fostered individual responsibility; in fact, it seems to foster social disparity and downplaying of the seriousness of crime
    - Maybe crime has penetrated the establishment

In fact, the arrangement is a variation of the classical *dispositio*. Following the introduction, the author briefly gives, in each argument, a broad "statement of fact" (*narratio*) summarizing current laws or economic conditions and immediately attacks them for the problems they cause, refuting their ostensible purpose (*refutatio*). Of course, the corrective introduction has already paved the way for such an arrangement.

The argument chain is thus as follows:

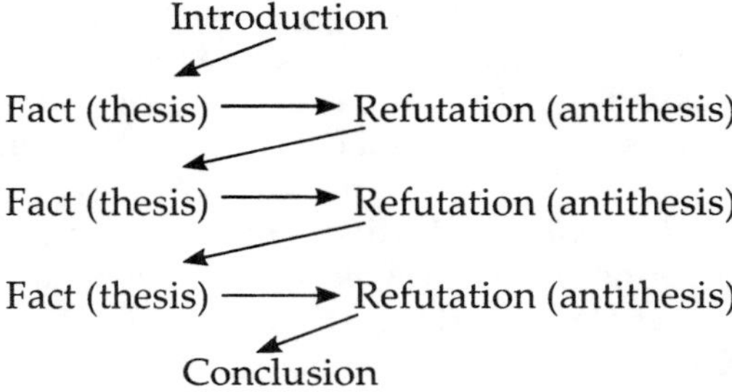

Argument Schema

Element	Description
Grounds	Poverty, unemployment, harsher sentences, increased crime
Claim	Failure of criminal justice and education systems
Warrant	Social democratic perspective
Backing	Political and social values
Qualifier	N/A
Rebuttal/restriction	N/A

Organizational relations: The binary organizational relation is easy to deduce from the arrangement and is twofold: thesis–antithesis and action or condition–consequence.

2. *Reading of TT*
Apart from typographical and spelling errors, no potential problems were noted at this stage.

3. *TT argument schema/arrangement/organizational relations*
There are a number of errors in the TT, but the complex and binary argument schemas are rendered adequately. All sections of the text contain components of the argument schema.

The thesis–antithesis relation is adequately rendered.

4. *Propositional functions/conjunctives/other inference indicators*
The selected passage illustrates the author's principal rhetorical techniques of repetition and amplification (reinforcement), which run through the article. They are manifested in the propositional functions themselves, with the author exemplifying and re-expressing key propositions before drawing a conclusion, the "clincher":

1. (para. 1) **Generalization**—poverty changes behaviour
2. **Elaboration**—it provokes antisocial behaviour but also makes traditional legal defence methods inaccessible
3. **Consequence**—inaccessibility of justice makes crime irresistible
4. **Elaboration**—example ("explosions d'insatisfaction populaire")
5. **Consequence**—conclusion = ineffectiveness and cost of traditional justice
6. (para. 2) **Elaboration** of proposition 2 as **generalization**—access to justice no longer a right for average citizen
7. **Elaboration**—legal profession apparently unconcerned
8. **Clarification**—lack of concern in spite of bar associations' statutes
9. **Consequence**—only rich can pay for legal defence
10. (para. 3) **Generalization**—reformulation of thesis expressed earlier in article, that poverty makes crime more attractive while at the same time exposing the less wealthy to harsher sentences
11. **Consequence**—conclusion: reformulation of thesis expressed earlier in article that corporations without a social conscience are globalizing misery and injustice

Markers are used sparingly to signpost the propositional development: two additives (*à cet égard, par exemple)* to introduce illustrations and a third additive (*or*) to introduce an elaboration.

The TT renders the propositional development adequately. The connections with the earlier co-text are preserved. However, two of the three conjunctives are misinterpreted: *bearing this in mind* for *à cet égard,* and *however* for *or,* which is not an adversative but an additive in this instance.

5. *Arguments*
In keeping with the corrective or refutational nature of the text, specific arguments are largely based on the pervasive topics of *relationship*

and *comparison*. The opposition of poverty to the justice system and of civilization ("société civilisée") to the justice system in the opening propositions is predicated on an argument from *contradiction* between the possible (with money) and the impossible (without money). This is reinforced by the *similarity* between money and justice in proposition 5. These relationships are mirrored and reinforced in the second paragraph through the *contrary* subtopic of *appearance* (bar associations' commitment to the public interest) and *reality* (their lack of concern for the average citizen) and the *cause/effect relationship* between the rich and access to legal counsel. In the third paragraph, the argument from *similarity* associates poverty with harsher sentences and globalization with poverty and injustice. The relationship and comparison arguments are backed up by examples (another argument by comparison) and by an argument from authority ("une évidence admise même par divers ministres provinciaux").

TT renders the arguments adequately.

6. *Figures*

Figures play a significantly greater role in this text than in the statistics documents. Indeed, they are a prime tool for reinforcing or amplifying the relationship and comparison arguments outlined above.

The translator does not preserve the extended biblical metaphor ("brandissent la foudre divine") in the first sentence. She does, however, preserve the metonymy ("celui qui crève de faim" for the concept of poverty), the rhetorical question and the antithesis "se faire justice ... la justice est hors de prix") in the third sentence, and the rhetorical question at the end of the first paragraph. The antithesis between wealthy and poor and the personification of law, justice, and crime in the subsequent paragraphs are maintained too. At the beginning of the third paragraph, the translator replaces the metaphor of the vise (*étau*) with that of the door but does not extend it as far as the author does in the ST.

7. *Narrative strategy*

The rhetorical questions and the frequent use of the third-person subject pronoun *on* serve as means of drawing the reader into the arguments, as a co-narrator with the author but also with society as a whole, seen as a helpless or complicit observer. The TT renders this technique adequately.

8. *Overall argumentation-centred TQA*

ARTRAQ Grid

Element	Translation assessment
Argument schema	Accurately rendered
Arrangement/ organizational relations	Accurately rendered
Propositional functions/ conjunctives/other inference indicators	Accurately rendered
Arguments	Accurately rendered
Figures	Metaphor inaccurately rendered
Narrative strategy	Accurately rendered

Results of the analysis of the TT against a broad range of argumentation parameters show that, in general, the translation meets most of the criteria and, in particular, those pertaining to core argument.

Quantitative TQA yields 1 major translation error, 34 minor translation errors, and 29 minor language errors in 1,668 words. The major error is based on the omission of a translation for "une autre relation avec l'argent," which results in a counterfactual statement in the TT. Within the sample, 9 minor translation errors and 7 minor language errors were detected.

The major error, which is outside the selected sample, does not undermine the reader's understanding of the argument schema: the relationship between economic systems and crime is reiterated and reinforced throughout the text and adequately conveyed in the TT. In short, the core argument is preserved.

In spite of the large number of minor errors, specific arguments and figures are accurately rendered, and only one deviation in propositional development was detected. So from an ARTRAQ perspective, the translation is satisfactory.

That being said, the text is for publication. A higher standard of target language quality would therefore be required.

Text 4

ST length: 1557 words
Text type: article for professional association periodical
Text mode: argumentative
Purpose: proffer an opinion on how society should deal with extreme right-wing parties and extreme religious sects
Again, the full text is assessed and a sample selected for special attention.

> SOURCE TEXT
>
> ***COMMENT RÉGLER LE PROBLÈME DES ATTEINTES AUX VALEURS ?***
>
> Deux débats peut-être plus apparentés qu'on ne le pense agitent l'Europe et, plus largement, la planète : l'entrée de l'extrême-droite dans un gouvernement autrichien de coalition; la recommandation acheminée au gouvernement français de dissoudre légalement l'Ordre du Temple solaire et l'Église de scientologie. Dans les deux cas, des États se demandent comment sanctionner les comportements qui sapent les valeurs collectives traditionnelles ou récemment conquises.
>
> **L'Autriche au pilori**
> Pour avoir accordé 27 % de ses suffrages à un parti d'extrême-droite et lui avoir ainsi ouvert les portes de la coalition gouvernementale, l'Autriche est soumise à l'heure actuelle aux reproches de ses partenaires européens et, plus largement, de la communauté internationale. Le score de 27 %, certes, est à peu près sans précédent dans le passé récent, mais cela ne range pourtant pas l'Autriche dans une catégorie à part. D'autres pays, depuis la France jusqu'au Danemark en passant par la paisible Norvège, subissent eux aussi la présence de partis aux penchants racistes assez clairement affichés. Si l'Autriche est vilipendée dans les diverses capitales européennes, ce n'est donc pas parce qu'elle est touchée comme les autres par la contamination xénophobe, mais parce qu'elle a été amenée à intégrer l'extrême-droite dans son gouvernement. C'est cela, et cela seulement, qui permet à ses partenaires européens de la blâmer en s'absolvant de leurs propres dérapages.
>
> Posée comme elle l'est par les capitales européennes, la question est d'ailleurs insoluble. Comment, en effet, autoriser l'extrême-

droite à faire campagne tout en lui interdisant de remporter la victoire ou de la partager avec un autre parti? Pourquoi les pays qui accusent l'Autriche n'ont-ils pas exprimé leurs craintes *avant* la campagne électorale? L'Algérie aussi a posé la question en ces termes et n'a pas encore trouvé la façon d'y répondre. Elle avait laissé le Front islamique du Salut participer à la campagne électorale, mais elle a ensuite empêché le FIS victorieux de profiter de sa victoire et de former le gouvernement. À la lumière de ces précédents, on devrait pourtant conclure ceci : pas plus contre un parti politique que contre un individu, on ne peut définir le crime de façon rétroactive. Si un parti n'était pas dans l'illégalité avant la campagne électorale, il ne peut pas l'être au lendemain du scrutin. D'où la nécessité de prévenir : si l'on ne veut pas que l'extrême-droite accède au pouvoir, il faut la mettre hors course avant que s'ouvre la sollicitation des suffrages. Pas facile.

L'ambiguïté des sectes

Un problème analogue se présente dans le domaine des sectes. Tôt ou tard, à peu près tous les États ont, en effet, à définir leur politique face à des organisations qui se qualifient de religions, mais que l'on soupçonne de constituer une menace contre l'ordre public et de pousser trop loin leurs atteintes à la dignité et à l'autonomie des personnes. L'analyse des situations concrètes ramène périodiquement à l'avant-scène l'alternative suivante : peut-on faire face aux abus des sectes avec la législation actuelle ou est-il indispensable de muscler cette législation et de la rendre plus claire? La France, pour ne parler que d'elle, vit à présent ce débat et hésite entre la rédaction préventive d'une loi moins poreuse ou plus spécialisée et les poursuites permises par les textes en vigueur. Comme dans le cas des partis indésirables, on constate qu'il n'est pas facile de reprocher aux sectes les comportements que semble autoriser la reconnaissance juridique de leur existence.

■ En amont ou en aval?

Peu importe la manière dont elle choisit de relever ces deux défis, une société est amenée à préciser en quoi consistent à ses yeux les crimes qui représentent une atteinte aux valeurs. Si, par exemple, une société interdit explicitement la propagande haineuse, elle opte pour une certaine protection et consent à un certain risque. Elle fait de la propagande haineuse un délit puisque, à ses yeux, il y a là un mal social si grave qu'on doit le réprimer, même si cela restreint le champ de la liberté d'expression et fait surgir la possibilité d'une censure. Si, à l'inverse, une société n'intègre pas à son code pénal un interdit visant directement la propagande haineuse, elle situe ailleurs l'équilibre souhaitable et loge ses valeurs dans une hiérarchie différente. Elle élargit, en effet, le champ ouvert à la libre expression, mais elle rend plus difficile la répression des déferlements haineux. Dans un cas, la société s'attache à l'indignité qu'est la propagande haineuse; dans l'autre hypothèse, la société fait confiance à ses lois générales. Dans les deux cas, la société révèle quelque chose d'important à propos de ses valeurs.

On voit à quel point il importe qu'une société choisisse entre l'amont et l'aval ou, plus précisément, qu'elle dise ce qu'elle entend régler en amont et comment elle croit pouvoir gérer l'aval. Elle ne peut pas, l'Algérie et l'Autriche sont là pour en témoigner, redresser brutalement en aval ce qu'elle a permis globalement en amont, refuser le verdict des urnes après avoir toléré la participation de Haider et de son Parti de la liberté à la campagne électorale. De la même manière, une société se complique l'existence — peut-être légitimement — si, en amont, elle accorde les privilèges d'un statut religieux à des sectes dont elle voudra ensuite, en aval, contester les comportements.

La réflexion française

Il est intéressant, dans cette perspective, de suivre la réflexion que mène la France à propos des sectes et d'établir le parallèle entre ses choix dans ce domaine et ceux qu'elle privilégie sur le terrain politique. Cela est d'autant plus intéressant que la France conserve encore, malgré des critiques croissantes, des institutions judiciaires qui intègrent difficilement notre présomption d'innocence, mais qui insistent davantage sur la parfaite laïcité de l'État.

Sur le terrain politique, la France subit depuis des années l'assaut d'une extrême-droite explicitement xénophobe et souvent à deux doigts de l'antisémitisme. ■ La réaction française la plus courante a été jusqu'à maintenant de laisser Le Pen participer aux campagnes électorales, mais de le traîner devant les tribunaux chaque fois (ou presque) qu'il poussait le bouchon trop loin. En d'autres termes, on n'interdit pas son parti, mais on recourt aux lois générales pour sanctionner les propos les moins tolérables de ce parti. Sans qu'on puisse affirmer qu'il y a lien de cause à effet entre cette stratégie et l'évolution subséquente, le fait est que Le Pen et ses excès ont perdu au fil des ans une part importante de leurs appuis électoraux.

La France, qui était en plus mauvaise posture que ses voisins, leur ressemble aujourd'hui davantage.

En ce qui concerne les sectes, la France semble tentée par une stratégie plus complexe. Elle marche sur des oeufs, comme le montre l'instabilité des techniques d'analyse et d'enquête. Qu'on en juge. En janvier 1996, un rapport parlementaire sur les sectes (Gest-Guyard) recommandait, ce qui n'était pas particulièrement audacieux, la création d'un *Observatoire interministériel sur les sectes*. Ce qui fut fait. L'Observatoire eut cependant une existence éphémère, sans doute parce qu'il adopta un ton insuffisamment ferme aux yeux des députés. Dès octobre 1998, l'Observatoire disparaissait, alors que surgissait à sa place la *Mission interministérielle de lutte contre les sectes*. On mesure la différence de perspective en voyant apparaître dans la désignation de la Mission, de manière d'ailleurs musclée, la notion de *lutte*.

On pouvait s'attendre à des recommandations d'une autre encre, d'autant plus que le président de la *Mission*, l'ancien ministre Alain Vivien, a déjà écrit, à titre personnel, un livre fort critique sur les sectes et qu'il préside depuis 1997 *le Centre Roger-Ikor contre les manipulations mentales*. On sait que l'écrivain Roger Ikor a créé ce centre après la mort de son fils, victime d'une secte, et on imagine dans quel esprit.

Or, voici que la *Mission* a remis un rapport (*Le Monde*, mercredi 9 février 2000) plein de nuances et de distinctions et débouchant sur une assez étonnante diversité de recommandations. En premier lieu, « une législation spécifique ne se justifie pas ». En deuxième lieu, « il convient d'adapter nos lois et nos règlements aux problèmes nouvellement posés ». En troisième lieu, comme pour préciser de quelle modernisation législative il est question, le rapport Vivien recommande au gouvernement français de se doter du pouvoir législatif de dissoudre deux organisations qu'il dénomme « sectes absolues » : l'Ordre du Temple solaire et l'Église de scientologie. En somme, quelque chose en amont et quelque chose en aval, quelque chose de nouveau dans le cadre général et quelque chose dans l'administration de la justice.

Un équilibre toujours précaire

Le dosage français n'est sans doute pas exportable tel quel. Il table sur des institutions et sur une culture civique particulières. Il a cependant le mérite de correspondre à une réflexion dont trop de sociétés, la nôtre comprise, prétendent faire l'économie.

Cette réflexion, l'évolution de notre époque la rend pourtant indispensable. Les groupes, qu'ils soient criminalisés ou religieux, informatiques ou paramilitaires, ont une liberté de mouvement — d'aucuns diraient une immunité — dont une société trop peu prudente risque de faire les frais. D'autre part, groupes et organisations doivent savoir en amont de leurs activités à quoi ils risquent de faire face en aval de la part des pouvoirs publics. Dès lors, les partis politiques et les organisations censément religieuses doivent obtenir de l'État ce qu'il leur faut de liberté et une définition claire de leurs responsabilités sociales.

L'équilibre sera toujours à redéfinir? Certes. Parce qu'il est le reflet de la vie.

TARGET TEXT

HOW SHOULD WE DEAL WITH CRIMES AGAINST VALUES?

Europe, and on a larger scale the entire planet, is facing *(T—shift)* two debates that may be more closely related than we think: the fact that the extreme right has formed a coalition government in Austria and the recommendation made to the French government to legally dissolve the Order of the Solar Temple and the Church of Scientology. In both cases, the States *(T—mistranslation)* are wondering how to sanction behaviour that undermines traditional or newly acquired collective values.

Austria in the Pillory

Its European partners and, more generally, the international community for the fact that 27 % of the vote went to an extreme-right party are currently censuring Austria, thereby opening the door to a coalition government. To be sure, 27 % is an *(T—omission)* un precedented *(L—typo)* figure in the recent past, but this does not put Austria into *(L—prepositional usage)* a class by itself. In other countries, including France, Denmark and even peaceful Norway, openly racist parties form part of the political scene. If the various European capitals are reviling Austria, it is not because Austria, like them, has xenophobic tendencies, but because it was forced *(T—shift)* to allow the extreme right to form part of the government. This, and only this, allows other European nations to censure Austria and turn a blind eye on their own excesses *(T—mistranslation)*.

Moreover, the question, as posed by European capitals, has no answer. Indeed, how can a country allow the extreme right to run a campaign and subsequently deny them the right to form a government outright or part of one? Why didn't the countries that are criticizing Austria now express their fears *before* the election campaign? Algeria, as well, has faced the same issue and has not yet come up with a solution. The country let the *Front islamique du Salut* (Islamic Salvation Front) participate in its election campaign, and subsequently prevented the victorious FIS from forming the government. In the light of these precedents, we should, however, come to the conclusion that we *(T—person)* cannot, in the case of either political parties or individuals, define crimes after the fact. If a party is not illegal before an election campaign, it cannot become so the day after the vote. Accordingly, we *(error repeated)* must use foresight: if we do not want the extreme right to come into power, it must be put out of the race before the electioneering starts. This is easier said than done.

The Case of Cults

Cults pose a similar problem. Indeed *(T—shift)*, at some point, nearly all States *(error repeated)* must define their policies regarding organizations, *(L—restrictive relative clause, omit comma)* which, on the surface, seem to qualify as religions, but are suspected of posing a threat to public order *(L—terminology)* and going too far in their attacks on the autonomy and dignity of people. The analysis of actual situations occasionally *(T—shift)* leads to the question *(T—mistranslation)*: Can we deal with the abuses of cults with existing legislation or must we clarify it and give it more muscle? France, among other countries, is currently facing this debate and is wavering between the preventive measure of drafting a more solid *(T—mistranslation)* and specific law and relying on the legal proceedings permitted by the statutory enactments currently in effect *(L—verbiage, redundancy)*. Just as in the case of undesirable political parties, we can see that it is difficult to criticize cults for behaviour that legal recognition of their existence *(T—omission)* authorizes.

■ Before or After the Fact?

No matter how a society chooses to meet these challenges, it must decide what exactly consitutes *(L—typo)* crimes against its particular values. If, for example, a society specifically outlaws hate propaganda, it opts for a certain protection, but it also consents to a certain risk. It makes hate propaganda a crime because, in its eyes, it poses such a social evil that it should be repressed, even if that curtails freedom of expression and may lead to the possibility *(L—redundancy)* of censorship. If, on the other hand, a society does not incorporate an anti-hate propaganda law into its criminal code, it opts for a different balance and places its values in an entirely different hierarchy. Having no specific law would effectively favour free expression, but at the cost of making it more difficult to contain outbursts of hatred. In the first hypothesis *(L—usage)*, society is according importance to the undesirableness *(T—mistranslation)* of propaganda; in the second, it is placing its confidence in its general laws. In both, society is revealing something important about its values.

You can see to what extent it is important that a society decide what it makes specific and what it leaves as general. Or, more precisely, what it says it intends to deal with before the fact and how it intends to deal with specific cases after the fact. It cannot, as the situations in Algeria and Austria demonstrate, brutally *(L—usage)* correct certain situations after the fact when they did nothing to stop the events that led up to them. A society cannot overturn the results of the polls after having tolerated the participation of Haider and the Freedom Party in the election campaign. In the same fashion, a society complicates its existence, perhaps legitimately, if it grants, before the fact, the status of legal religious order to cults and then, after the fact, wants to challenge their actions.

The French Reflection

Using *(L—usage)* this perspective, it is interesting to follow the French train of thought *(T—mistranslation)* concerning cults and to establish a parallel between its choices in this area and those it favours *(T—shift)* in the field of politics. This is made even more so *(T—mistranslation)* by the fact that France still maintains, despite mounting criticism, judicial institutions that integrate with difficulty our presumption of innocence, but rather place the emphasis on the complete separation of Church and State.

For several years now, on the political front, France has been under assault from an explicitly xenophobic extreme right that often stops just short of anti-Semitism. ■ The most common French tactic to date has been to let Le Pen participate in election campaigns, and prosecute him each time (or nearly) *(L—usage)* he goes too far. In other words, France has not outlawed his party, but rather turns to general legislation to sanction its less tolerable comments. While a cause and effect *(L—hyphenation)* relationship between this strategy and subsequent events cannot be established, the fact remains that Le Pen and his excesses have lost an *(L—typo)* large share of their political support over the years. France, which was in a worse state than its neighbours, now more closely resembles them.

When it comes to cults, France seems to be leaning towards a more complex strategy. The instability of its survey *(T—mistranslation)* and analysis techniques shows the country is walking on eggs. Let's take a closer look at the situation. In January 1996, a parliamentary report on cults (Gest-Guyard) recommended that the *Observatoire interministériel sur les cultes* (interministerial committee to monitor cults) be created, a not particularly daring move. This was done. However, the *Observatoire* had a short-lived existence, no doubt because it did not take a firm enough stand in the ministers' *(T—mistranslation)* eyes. In October 1998, it disappeared, and was replaced with the *Mission interministérielle de lutte contre les cultes* (interministerial task force to combat cults). The change in attitude, to a tougher stance, *(L—erroneous parenthesis)* can be seen in the use of *lutte* in the *Mission's* title.

We could have expected some recommendations of a totally different nature, for, among other reasons *(T—mistranslation)*, Alain Vivien, the former minister, privately *(T—mistranslation)* authored a book severely critical of cults and has also served as president of the *Centre Roger-Ikor contre les manipulations mentales* (Roger Ikor centre against mental manipulation) since 1997. Roger Ikor founded the centre on the death of his son, victim of a cult, and we can imagine in what frame of mind *(L—omission, syntax)*.

And yet, *(L—punctuation)* the *Mission* tabled a report (*Le Monde*, Wednesday, February 9, 2000) full of distinctions and nuances, making some astonishingly diverse recommendations. First, it stated that specific legislation is not justified. It added that it would be preferable for France to adapt its laws and regulations to deal with recently arising problems *(L—usage)*. It then went on to specify exactly what kind of legislative updating was required. The Vivien Report recommended that the French government grant itself the legislative power to dissolve two organizations that it labelled "absolute cults": the Order of the Solar Temple and the Church of Scientology. In summary *(L—usage)*, something both before and after the fact, something new in both the general framework and the administration of justice.

An Ever Precarious *(L—hyphenation)* **Equilibrium** *(L—terminology)* The French solution is undoubtedly non-exportable as it stands. It is based on a specific civil culture and *(T—omission)* institutions. However, it has the merit of corresponding with *(L—prepositional usage)* the way that too many societies, including ours, claim to run their economy *(Major T—mistranslation of metaphor)*. The manner in which our era is unfolding, however, is making this way of thinking a necessity. Whether they be criminal or religious, computer-based or paramilitary, groups enjoy a freedom of movement, some would even say an immunity, that is likely to cost unwary societies dearly. On the other hand, groups and organizations should know before the fact the price they will have to pay to *(T—mistranslation)* public powers *(L—terminology)* after the fact. Political parties and *(T—omission)* religious organizations should, from this point forward, have the State give them what they need in the way of liberty and a clear definition of their social responsibilities.

Will we constantly have to redefine the equilibrium? Of course. Equilibrium is a reflection of life.

1. *ST argument schema/arrangement/organizational relations*

Arrangement

1. **Introduction**: *inquisitive* in type, piquing the reader's interest by suggesting a relationship, in terms of social values, between two distinct situations and alluding, in very general terms, to the dilemma faced by governments in dealing with groups that attack mainstream values
2. **Statement of facts 1**: the emergence of the extreme right-wing Freedom Party in Austria and of a fundamentalist party in Algeria and national and international reaction
3. **Conclusion 1**: crime cannot be defined retroactively
4. **Reiteration of dilemma**, with specific reference to sects and to France
5. **General statement of alternatives** and **dilemma**: protection vs. freedom of expression
6. **Reiteration of Conclusion 1**
7. **Statement of facts 2**: solutions devised by France to both dilemmas (extreme-right and sects)
8. **Reformulation of Conclusion 1**

Again, the arrangement is a variation of the classical *dispositio*, but the argumentative approach is not refutation but a value-based judgment of facts. Following the general introduction, outlining the dilemma facing certain governments, the author presents the facts pertaining to the political dilemma facing Austria and Algeria (*narratio*) before drawing a conclusion on what the correct approach to the dilemma should be (*confirmatio*). The author then reformulates the dilemma with reference to religious sects in France (*narratio*) before presenting alternative solutions to what he sees as the generic dilemma—the opposition between repression of "social evil" and freedom of speech and thought—and reformulating the initial conclusion (*confirmatio*). The *narratio–confirmatio* process is then used a third time.

Argument Schema

Element	Description
Grounds	Events and responses in Austria, Algeria, and France
Claim	Legal and ethical impossibility of declaring groups illegal after the fact
Warrant	Government's legislative mandate
Backing	Values of coherence and consistency in law
Qualifier	N/A
Rebuttal/restriction	N/A

Organizational relations: The binary organizational relation can be deduced from the arrangement: evidence (illustration)–conclusion.

2. *Reading of TT*

Examination of the TT reveals no obvious problems of coherence. Some typographical errors were detected. All sections of the ST contain components of the argument schema.

3. *TT argument schema/arrangement/organizational relations*

There are a number of errors in the TT, but the mistranslation in the second sentence of the penultimate paragraph is more significant than the others. The author recommends the French solution to the problem of religious sects and states that too many countries are ignoring this approach. He then emphasizes the recommendation by saying that the solution is becoming a necessity in today's world. Because of the translator's misunderstanding of "faire l'économie," the TT sentence is incoherent, implying that many countries have adopted such an approach, that it is related to management of the economy, and that it is inappropriate ("too many").

The proposition conveyed is part of the claim, and the translation undermines the development of the final claim argument. However, the arguments in the rest of the final paragraph, and in particular the reference to the necessity of the French solution in the following sentence, are translated with sufficient accuracy to compensate for the incoherence.

The evidence–conclusion relation is adequately rendered in the TT.

4. *Propositional functions/conjunctives/other inference indicators*
The selected passage, "En amont ou en aval," illustrates the author's principal rhetorical technique of presenting a dilemma and then drawing a conclusion from it:

1. **Generalization** 1—definition of crime against values required
2. **Elaboration** 1—example: specific legislation outlawing hate propaganda
3. **Qualification** 1—contradictory example: no specific legislation
4. **Generalization** 2 from Elaboration 1 (*Dans un cas...*)
5. **Generalization** 3 from Qualification 1/also Qualification of Generalization 2 (*dans l'autre hypothèse...*)
6. **Generalization** 4 from generalizations 2 and 3, connecting with issue of values raised in Generalization 1 (*Dans les deux cas...*)
7. **Generalization** 5 from generalizations 2, 3, and 4, connecting with requirement stated in Generalization 1 (*On voit à quel point...*)
8. **Clarification** of Generalization 5: required coherence of definitions before and after the fact (*Elle ne peut pas...*)
9. **Elaboration** of Clarification through example (*...l'Algérie et l'Autriche...*)

10. **Elaboration** of Clarification through example (*...statut religieux à des sectes...*)

The dilemma is conveyed in part through the qualification functions of certain propositions, and the predominance of the unifying idea, or recommendation, regarding coherence in lawmaking is reflected in the recurrence of the generalization function.

Adversative markers are used to signpost the dilemma: *à l'inverse; Dans un cas/dans l'autre hypothèse.* Additives are used to signpost elaboration and generalization: *par exemple, de la même manière.* Note also that the focus on the coherence requirement and the similarity of the situations selected as examples is reflected in the use of "Dans les deux cas" and "de la même manière." In the same paragraph, "On voit à quel point" is an inference indicator, inviting the reader to relate the preceding argument to the initial thesis of the article.

In the TT, *effectively* is a slight mistranslation of *en effet*, and "In the first hypothesis" is unidiomatic and fails to preserve the argument development signposted by the repetition of *cas*. Otherwise, TT renders the propositional development adequately.

5. *Arguments*

The text involves the examination of a dilemma, or a choice between two alternatives, neither of which is ideal. Taking specific examples (argument by *comparison*) as a base, the author uses *induction* to express the dilemma in general statements and to formulate alternatives and recommendations. The general statements involve a complex of arguments from *definition, contraries, contradiction,* and *circumstance*, as illustrated in the selected passage.

> **Before or After the Fact?**
> No matter how a society chooses to meet these challenges, it must decide what exactly constitutes crimes against its particular values [**definition**]. If, for example, a society specifically outlaws hate propaganda, it opts for a certain protection, but it also consents to a certain risk [**contraries** *of safety and risk*]. It makes hate propaganda a crime because, in its eyes, it poses such a social evil that it should be repressed, even if that curtails freedom of expression and may lead to the possibility of censorship [**comparison/degree**: *hate propaganda a greater evil than curtailment of freedom of expression*; **relationship/cause and effect**: *potential undesirable consequences of specific law*]. If, on the other

> hand, a society does not incorporate an anti-hate propaganda law into its criminal code, it opts for a different balance and places its values in an entirely different hierarchy [**contraries**: *reversal of judgment on* **comparison/degree** *components*]. Having no specific law would effectively favour free expression, but at the cost of making it more difficult to contain outbursts of hatred [**relationship/cause and effect** *reformulated*]. In the first hypothesis, society is according importance to the undesirableness of propaganda; in the second, it is placing its confidence in its general laws [**contraries** *of specific and general*]. In both, society is revealing something important about its values [**relationship/sign and cause**: *laws and values*].
>
> You can see to what extent it is important that a society decide what it makes specific and what it leaves as general. Or, more precisely, what it says it intends to deal with before the fact and how it intends to deal with specific cases after the fact. It cannot, as the situations in Algeria and Austria demonstrate, brutally correct certain situations after the fact when they did nothing to stop the events that led up to them [*combination of argument from* **contraries** *of acceptance and rejection and argument from* **circumstance**: *past fact (acceptance) and future fact (rejection)*]. A society cannot overturn the results of the polls after having tolerated the participation of Haider and the Freedom Party in the election campaign [*argument from* **circumstance** *illustrated by argument from* **comparison** *(example)*]. In the same fashion, a society complicates its existence, perhaps legitimately, if it grants, before the fact, the status of legal religious order to cults and then, after the fact, wants to challenge their actions [*argument from* **circumstance** *illustrated by double argument from* **comparison** *(example and similarity of examples)*].

This shows the number, complexity, and coherence of the individual arguments in the TT, which, in spite of several transfer and target language defects, renders the ST arguments adequately.

6. *Figures*

The extended spatial metaphor *en amont/en aval* in the selected ST passage plays an integral role in conveying the requirement of consistency in lawmaking. The translator elects not to produce an equivalent spatial metaphor in English, conveying instead the time-based denotative meaning of the relationship between legal events. The translation is adequate. On the other hand, the major translation error is, in fact, due to a failure to recognize a finance metaphor.

7. *Narrative strategy*

The rhetorical question, used to draw the reader into the arguments in the preceding text, is less frequent here. The pronoun *on*, translated variously as *we* and *you*, is used to the same extent, however. In this case, the reader is enlisted as co-narrator and co-analyst, instead of being a passive observer. The TT renders this technique adequately.

On the other hand, the translator provides no translation for the important qualifier *censément* in the noun phrase "les organisations censément religieuses" (third line from end). The adverb reveals the author's opinion of sects, but the opinion is not conveyed in the TT.

8. *Overall argumentation-centred TQA*

ARTRAQ Grid

Element	**Translation assessment**
Argument schema	Accurately rendered
Arrangement/ organizational relations	Accurately rendered
Propositional functions/conjunctives/ other inference indicators	Most accurately rendered
Arguments	Accurately rendered
Figures	Accurately rendered
Narrative strategy	Accurately rendered

Results of the analysis of TT against a broad range of argumentation parameters show that, in general, the translation meets all the criteria and, in particular, those pertaining to core argument.

The major error does not undermine the reader's understanding of the argument schema because the central idea, or claim, is expressed on several occasions and rendered accurately elsewhere in TT.

At a more microtextual level, in spite of the large number of minor errors, specific arguments and figures are accurately rendered, and only one deviation in propositional development was detected.

That being said, the text is for publication. A higher standard of target language quality would therefore be required.

Quantitative TQA yields 1 major translation error, 24 minor translation errors, and 22 minor language errors in 1,557 words. Had the evaluation been based solely on the selected passage, which is about 400 words in length, the major error would no longer be a factor and the text, based on 9 minor errors, might well be considered fully acceptable under both Sical (equivalent to B rating under old Sical III grid) and GTS (under 5 minor translation errors).

5.3. Comparative summary of results

The following table highlights the results of the assessments conducted on the four texts and in particular the overall assessments generated by the ARTRAQ and microtextual models.

The table shows the following:

- Only in one case (text 2) do the ARTRAQ and quantitative-microtextual assessments clearly generate the same overall judgment. In the other three cases, the overall quantitative-microtextual assessment, or rating, hinges on the number of minor errors alone. Moreover, in two of those, the number of minor language errors might well have tipped the balance toward a lower rating (C under the old Sical III grid). Note that the Sical and GTS models do not weight translation errors more heavily than language errors.

- In all cases, major errors (as defined under the Sical model), some of which adversely affected the reader's understanding of the core argument, were detected immediately outside the selected sample. In three cases (1, 3, and 4), they were not deemed to adversely affect the argument schema under ARTRAQ.

- Unless a major error is detected, the quantitative-microtextual rating has to be based on number of errors (texts 1, 3, and 4). This poses a problem particularly with respect to texts 3 and 4, which could be considered "borderline" cases because of the relatively few translation errors.

Comparative Summary Table of Assessments

Text result	ARTRAQ	Rationale	Quantitative-microtextual result (based on sample)	Rationale
1 Statistical report	Unsatisfactory	Grounds mistranslated, in large part through failure to render conjunctives and thereby clarify propositional functions appropriately; therefore, argument schema not preserved in TT	10T, 7L Note: 1 maj. T outside sample	No. of errors
2 Statistical report	Unsatisfactory	Grounds, claims, narrative strategy misinterpreted; therefore, argument schema not preserved in TT	1 maj. T, 6T, 7L Note: 2 maj. T outside sample	No. of errors
3 Crime article	Satisfactory	Argument schema rendered	9T, 7L Note: 1 maj. T outside sample	No. of errors
4 Crime article	Satisfactory	Argument schema rendered	4T, 5L (Fully acceptable, B, under old Sical III, and under GTS guidelines) Note: 1 maj. T outside sample	No. of errors

- ARTRAQ, on the other hand, is largely non-quantitative and explanatory. The comparative results show that differences in rating between ARTRAQ and the microtextual models are attributable to argument schema analysis and, more specifically, the fact ARTRAQ provides a rationale for the major error.

We will revisit this table in chapter seven, after refining the model.

CHAPTER SIX

REFINING THE MODEL

6.1. Introduction

The next step in the modelling process is to determine, on the basis of our analysis, what changes or refinements are required to optimize the model. I will also be examining the potential for incorporating a rating scale in the model, and it is the issue of rating that will lead into our exploration of the translation quality standard as such in chapter seven.

6.2. Overall and field/use-specific TQA

6.2.1. *Findings*

Based on the analysis, we can draw the following conclusions about the degree to which the model is comprehensive—that is, incorporates a broad range of parameters and can generate normative statements about overall quality and discrete qualitative factors.

(a) The range of parameters (argument schema, arrangement, and organizational relations; propositional functions, conjunctives, and other inference indicators; arguments; figures of speech; and narrative strategy) is broad enough to encompass most, if not all, defects in the transfer of meaning. Even a single specialized term can be related to an argumentation (reasoning) parameter, as in the case of *automobiles* in text 1.

(b) In other words, the advantage of the ARTRAQ parameters is that they serve to situate within their co-text and context defects treated conventionally from a microtextual perspective. The model forces the evaluator to seek argumentation linkages between the word, phrase, and sentence and the surrounding text and context and to focus on the *message* at all levels.

(c) That being said, not all terminology and official title defects, omissions, and other mistranslations will have an impact on the quality of a translation as assessed by means of the ARTRAQ model. Furthermore, at this stage it provides for any evaluation of target language quality (style, usage, morphology, syntax, and typography) only in certain instances. We have seen that under one model, the Ontario GTS (see 1.1.1), major language defects can be characterized as transfer defects for TQA purposes because they hinder or prevent the reader's understanding of the text, and our examples of defects in the rendering of ST narrative strategy in text 2 show how morphosyntactic structures are critical to argumentation. For other aspects of language quality, however, the model would have to be expanded in some way.

(d) The model provides for an overall assessment of translation quality to the extent (1) that its combination of discourse-based analysis and sample TQA is valid, and (2) that the parameters can be used to make distinctions among translation quality levels. Further conclusions on its potential in this regard will be made in a later section, where the definition of seriousness of errors will be considered.

(e) Consideration was given to including "arrangement" (*dispositio*) as a parameter. Testing indicated that analysis of arrangement is useful as an explanatory tool—that is, for grasping the overall development of the text—but does not highlight discrete differences between ST and TT. It can therefore be dropped as a core assessment parameter and used where required for specific explanatory purposes.

(f) The analysis of organizational relations necessarily yields results similar, if not identical, to that of argument schema. For example, evidence (part of the evidence–conclusion relation) in text 4 is equivalent to grounds in the argument schema. Again, this parameter can be reserved for specific purposes.

(g) Figures of speech proved to be relevant only in the legal affairs/popular criminology texts. On the other hand, narrative strategy was relevant in the statistics texts.

(h) The linkage between propositional functions (coherence) and conjunctives/inference indicators (cohesion) is strong and is of considerable explanatory and informational value, so both parameters should be retained in the generic model.

6.3. Comparison of ARTRAQ and quantitative-microtextual TQA in terms of quality of information

6.3.1. *Findings*

Here, we broach the raison d'être of the proposed model: its informational value and its validity.

(a) The defect–argumentation linkage enhances the explanatory force of TQA. In characterizing the defect, the evaluator necessarily examines it in terms of deviation from the argumentation in the source text and is in a position to define the problem accordingly. Thus what is conventionally labelled a *mistranslation, significant mistranslation, major mistranslation, faux sens, contresens,* or *glissement de sens* will also be characterized in terms of its impact on reasoning not only at the subsentence level but also at higher levels, including that of the text.

(b) By extension, the model also links assessment to the objectives of the ST author, the target text, and the client, where these objectives are known or can be extrapolated from the texts in question. As Larose has pointed out, in order for TQA to be valid—that is, to generate an accurate assessment of what it purports to evaluate—it must be teleological. Evidence was adduced in chapter three to show that the objective of persuasion through reasoning, argumentation, and rhetoric was a consideration in instrumental texts in all fields. The testing has shown how the model provides a means of evaluating quality in terms of the degree of preservation of the persuasive tools of the ST. In short, the originality of the model as a means of extracting information resides in its potential for evaluating the translation unit, of whatever size it may be, as part of a broader speech act.

(c) The testing shows that an argumentation-centred TQA can yield valid theory-based results differing from those generated by the quantitative model because of the application of Toulmin's argument schema model. The six-point structure contributes two vital components to my proposal, providing a means of determining (1) the essential elements of a text's "message," and (2) the essential sections of that text. Specifically, it gives us, first, a theoretical basis for the identification of major/critical defects (to be differentiated later) as those mistranslations that hinder or prevent the reader's understanding of the *grounds, claims, warrants, backing, rebuttals* (*exceptions, restrictions*) and possibly *qualifiers* in the text under consideration. In other words, these are the "essential parts of the message" of the text as a whole, and mistranslation of one or more of them means that the translation is inadequate on the dimension of transfer, *unless the argument schema component is correctly rendered elsewhere in the TT and the defect is thus compensated for.* Second, Toulmin's model enables us to make an important distinction between "representative" and "essential" sections or samples of a text. A "representative" sample does not necessarily contain an essential part of the message of the text *as a whole,* and what is deemed to be essential within the sample may be of secondary importance within the entire discourse. Application of Toulmin's model ensures that only passages containing the key components of the argument schema are selected for TQA purposes and that, therefore, only defects pertaining to those components can be assessed as major or critical.

The consequences are significant. Seriousness of defect can no longer be solely microtext-based; it is a function of the translation unit's relationship with the argument schema. In addition, the evaluator is no longer left to make an empirical judgment, based on his or her own experience or opinion, on what is essential in a given passage or text. Nor is the evaluator left to surmise as to the potential consequences of defects for the client—a tall order unless a very detailed work statement is available and the intended use of the translation is known. The evaluator has been given a theoretical basis and a set of clear parameters for the assessment of major/critical defects. This in itself should be particularly helpful in countering the charges of evaluative subjectivity that are often levelled by professional translators and theorists alike. Furthermore, the fact that the scope of critical/major errors has been clearly circumscribed for the evaluator means that the potential for error of judgment is kept to a minimum and TQA reliability is enhanced.

(d) As a result, the argumentation-centred TQA model yielded a different assessment of major/critical defects on several occasions, based on relative impact on the argument schema. I also found that a combination of defects, though perhaps anodyne when considered individually, was sufficient to compromise the argument schema: the specific cases involved a series of mistranslated conjunctives and elements of narrative strategy. To use Sperber's and, following his lead, Gutt's terminology of the pragmatics of communication, the efficiency of the process is significantly impaired in the text with the mistranslated conjunctives: the reader must make undue effort to interpret the message because the signposts are not there to guide him or her. In short, the concept of "major error," once redefined on the basis of Toulmin's model, will be based not on an arbitrary, absolutist notion of correctness at the word or even sentence level but on the target translation unit's function within, and contribution to, the core argument of the text.

(e) ARTRAQ thus serves to circumvent the "borderline case" problem left intact by quantification of error, as we saw in text 4, because it provides a theory-based rationale for the evaluator's decision.

(f) As the definitions of error presented in chapter four show, usability of a product is contingent on the absence of major/critical defects, and in a translation context *adequacy* and *deliverability* have been substituted for *usability* to characterize work meeting the same quality criterion. The advantage of the criterion is that the problem of defect quantification is circumvented, as we saw in our analysis of text 1. We thus have a theoretical basis for a preliminary, binary rating scale.

Preliminary ARTRAQ Rating Scale

Grade	Definition
Satisfactory	No defect affecting argument schema
Unsatisfactory	At least one defect affecting argument schema

(g) The rating scale is embryonic. It needs to be refined in light of requirements for assessment against other factors (target language, terminology, format, text type, intended use, etc.).

(h) Last but not least, the testing yielded some interesting observations on sampling. First, while scanning the full ST and then the TT can lead to the identification of potential problems that can be followed up with closer analysis, it does not appear to do so in all cases. Second, while the same initial steps certainly enable the evaluator to identify the argument schema of the ST and the sections that contain components thereof, the schema may span the whole text, as we saw in the statistics texts. Does this mean that in such cases, one has no choice but to assess the quality of the whole translation in order to produce a valid ARTRAQ assessment? It probably does. However, the constraints of time being what they are, reading the TT to detect problem areas and ensuring assessment of passages that are not just representative but contain key components of the argument schema should provide for efficiency while offering a higher degree of validity than conventional models.

6.4. Refinements

Based on the above findings, we will make a number of changes to the model in the interests of efficiency, validity, and reliability or stability.

6.4.1. *Parameters and grid*

(a) Drop "arrangement" and "organizational relations" as core parameters.

(b) Drop figures of speech as a core parameter in the TQA grid, but include it as a field-specific parameter in an extended model, to be developed below.
(c) Incorporate other parameters (terminology, style, usage, typography, etc.) according to text type, field, and intended use.

6.4.2. *Seriousness of error*

(a) Establish a threefold distinction among *critical*, *major*, and *minor* defects, as indicated in the industrial quality-control literature. Application of Toulmin's argument schema has yielded a new concept of a defect that seriously undermines the usability of the translation because it impairs the central reasoning of the text. Furthermore, I found that not all defects considered major under the quantitative-microtextual model corresponded to the new concept. Accordingly, my proposal is that

- defects impairing translation of the argument schema be characterized as *critical*;
- other transfer defects conventionally considered major (*contresens*, *charabia*) be characterized as *major* in the ARTRAQ model and be deemed not to render the translation unusable;
- other transfer defects be characterized as *minor*.

The critical defect would correspond to the text-level misinterpretation identified by Bensoussan and Rosenhouse (see 1.1.1) with reference to student translations. I will broaden the application of the three levels of defect to industry translations by developing definitions for each of them in line with argumentation theory.
(b) The modified and extended grid and the above characterizations will be the starting point for a rating scale.

6.4.3. *Full-text assessment versus sampling*

Reading the complete translation to identify problem areas and restricting detailed TQA to passages containing argument schema components will save time and will be incorporated into the ARTRAQ procedure. That being said, application of the model showed that any text, however long or short, contains grounds, claims, warrants, and so on. Therefore, pre-delivery quality assurance would ideally entail detailed examination of all passages containing key elements of the argument schema, precisely to detect and eradicate the serious defects of which, according to Gouadec (1989b: 56), even the most competent translators are capable.

6.4.4. *The revised model*

We can now finalize our ARTRAQ grid according to two sets of parameters: core and field- or use-specific. The core parameters will apply to all instrumental translations, whatever their end use may be and whatever subject field is involved. The field- or specific-use parameters will be activated at the evaluator's discretion, in light of the contract or work statement at hand, the field of specialization, and the intended use of the translation.

Core Argumentation-Centred TQA Parameters

Element
Argument schema
Propositional functions/conjunctives/other inference indicators
Arguments
Narrative strategy

The field- or use-specific parameters typically selected by the evaluator would include terminology, figures of speech, format, and target language quality. In fact, it would no doubt be appropriate to subdivide target language quality into *style, usage and grammar,* and *typography,* since their relevance and importance varies with field and use. For example, style—in which we include issues of redundancy, repetition, concision, and plain language—may be of scant consequence for the translation of an administrative report but is of considerable importance in the translation of directives and instructions. Likewise, typographical errors may not be a major factor in assessing the quality of internal documents but will have major consequence in signage, as the real-life example below (a sign in a government building in Ottawa in the early nineties) illustrates.

Elevators
Ascenceurs

In the case of an internal report for information purposes, terminology and format may be important, but matters of target language quality may be secondary; accordingly, the translation will be assessed against the first two but not against the target language parameters. At the same time, it must be borne in mind that defects in terms of non-core parameters may have already been factored into the assessment against the core parameters. For example, a misrepresentation of the official title of the organization at the centre of the argumentation in a policy document may strike directly at the quality of the argument schema in the TT.

6.4.5. *Development of a rating scale*

We want to continue working toward our objective of a TQA model that reduces quantification of defects (errors) to a minimum. We also want to avoid the situation obtaining in other models, where all types of minor error were given the same weight.

The multicriteria model proposed by Larose (1994: 369) makes it possible for the evaluator to reflect the relative importance of each parameter in the overall, final assessment. It requires that each parameter be assigned a specific weight prior to assessment and that the quality level for a specific parameter, as determined by the evaluator, be weighted accordingly in the establishment of an overall rating.

Larose draws inspiration for his model from a criteria-based analysis published by Nida, in which each of three translations of the same original is assessed against six key parameters, called "isomorphs"—referential meaning, rime, concision of lines of poetry, and so on. Each translation is assessed a plus (+), minus (–), or plus/minus (±) to indicate its success against each parameter. Although no judgment is made as to which translation is the best, a subtraction of the total number of –'s from the total number of +'s would be one way of establishing a list by descending order of quality. There is no question of counting the number of individual errors under a given parameter; a text-level assessment is the goal. According to Nida, "Isomorphs are essentially a way of looking at the basic problem of equivalence. But what is important about isomorphs is that they force the analyst to specify the formal and semantic features in such a way as to measure and describe the degrees of conformity. *Since isomorphs always come in sets of features, they force literary critics and translators to think in terms of patterns and not in terms of isolated resemblances and differences*" (Larose

1998: 179; my emphasis). In short, Nida is proposing an overall assessment not of the translation as a whole, but of the translation *against each parameter and in terms of its overall manifestation.* Note that Nida does not issue a final comparative assessment and, accordingly, does not propose any weighting formula.

Larose's multicriteria analytical table, like Nida's, is designed for a criterion-referenced assessment, and specifically for evaluation of student translations and candidates' performance in recruitment and promotion examinations, but he builds into his model an explicit recognition of the varying importance of the parameters. One proposed framework described by Larose is as shown below (Larose 1994: 369):

Criterion	**1**	**2**	**3**	**4**	**5**	**6**	**Total**
Weighting / Translation	10	7	7	8	9	9	
A	7/70	6/42	8/56	7/56	4/36	5/45	305
B	6/60	5/35	9/63	6/48	6/54	7/63	323
C	4/40	8/56	1/7	7/56	5/45	9/81	285

Here, the top line, "Criterion," represents the different parameters against which translation quality is to be assessed: transfer, terminology, typography, and so on. Each criterion is then weighted from 1 to 10, depending on its importance to translation quality. The evaluator assesses each translation (A, B, C) against all criteria, giving it a mark out of 10 for each criterion and multiplying that mark by the weighting factor: thus, translation A rates a mark of 7 against criterion 1 (which has a weighting factor of 10) and thus earns 70 points (7 x 10) toward its total score, which is made up of the sum of the points earned against each criterion.

Adapting Larose's framework to criterion-referenced TQA, we can devise an appropriate weighting formula and a grid incorporating core and field- or use-specific parameters. Our first objective is to establish an appropriate unit of measurement. The above rating system may work well for comparisons, but in general evaluators are more used to basing grades on percentages, which are relatively easy to calculate. The

Ontario Government Translation Services has taken this approach (see 1.1.1). It is also important to work with a measurement tool that yields clear "mathematical" differences in quality. In this regard, Fatzer and Stora relate the unit of measurement in pre-delivery quality control to psychological and cognitive development:

> We all experienced quantity for the first time by counting with our ten fingers and thumbs. This anchored certain images in our subconscious—specifically, anything above 1 is perceived as being big, and anything below 1 is perceived as being small.
>
> ... Therefore, when we consider the measurement of quality in terms of dysfunction or non-conformity, it is better for us to select a unit so that the result of the measurement is higher than 10. Then we will have the impression that the degree of dysfunction or non-conformity is high and we will be tempted to take action. Conversely, a unit selected so that the measurement ... is expressed by a number lower than 1 will give us the impression that the degree of dysfunction or non-conformity is low and that there is no reason to be concerned. (Fatzer and Stora, 1990: 221; our translation)

The same reasoning can be applied to translation quality assessments, since their ultimate objective, too, is to bring about improvement in quality.

It therefore makes sense to base the weighting factors on percentages. We therefore assume that a translation with no defects is worth 100%. Since we have already established that a "satisfactory" translation preserves the argument schema of the ST, we can give a fixed percentage (30%) for this parameter: any defect at this level results in a 0% score for the parameter. Thus, in percentage terms, the "satisfactory" translation scores at least 71%. The evaluator would decide what portion of the remaining 100% was represented by the selected parameters, which could include other core ARTRAQ parameters, and express that portion as a decile. The evaluator would then rate translation quality for each parameter, using a rating system commonly applied in criterion- and **norm-referenced** assessment: 10 = excellent; 8 = very satisfactory; 6 = satisfactory; 4 = fair; 2 = poor. The resulting weighted TQA grid would include parameters from the core ARTRAQ grid and from the field- or end-use-specific grid.

For example, the weighted ARTRAQ grid for text 3, the first of the highly argumentative popular criminology articles, translation of which was for publication purposes, might be based on high weights for target-language parameters and include the "arguments" parameter from the core grid:

Argumentative Article (for Publication) Weighted ARTRAQ Grid

Parameter	Weight (/10)	Minimum requirement	Quality (/10)	Rationale	Score (/100)
Argument schema	3	(10) 30			
Arguments	2	(8) 16			
Style, usage, and grammar	3	(8) 24			
Typography	2	(8) 16			
Total	10	**86**			

In the statistics texts, in which narrative strategy and propositional functions and conjunctives have proven to be of significance in the assessment process and which contain an abundance of specialized terms, the weighted grid might include these three parameters.

Statistical Report Weighted ARTRAQ Grid

Parameter	Weight (/10)	Minimum requirement	Quality (/10)	Rationale	Score (/100)
Argument schema	3	(10) 30			
Propositional functions/ conjunctives/other inference indicators	2	(8) 16			
Narrative strategy	2	(6) 12			
Typography	1	(6) 6			
Terminology	2	(8) 16			
Total	10	**80**			

Because ARTRAQ can now serve to isolate and weight specific criteria (parameters) for assessment, the model seems to offer greater potential for content validity—that is, for covering the broad range of skills necessary for actual translation performance—than do conventional quantitative-microtextual models, based as they are on only transfer/language and major/minor error (CTIC and J2450 do, however, provide for a weighting of error types).

ARTRAQ is also modular in that it is adaptable to specific fields and end uses. As such, it makes it possible to focus the assessment on the criterion or criteria of interest and ensure the validity of assessments across the various conditions of production. Appendix 1 contains a model assessment illustrating use of the weighted TQA grid.

The mathematical model itself is relatively straightforward, requiring simple calculations. The next step is more challenging, however. For ARTRAQ to become a useful criterion-referenced tool and at the same time serve as a quality standard, the scores must be given a value and a description in relation to a standard; labels such as "excellent," "very satisfactory," "good," and "fair" may serve a purpose in making comparisons among performances but do not adequately describe level of quality in relation to a standard or degree of progress toward a standard or quality objective.

CHAPTER SEVEN

ARTRAQ AND DEVELOPMENT OF A STANDARD

7.1. Introduction

The review of the literature in chapter one highlighted the fact that theorists and researchers in translation studies have, by and large, eschewed actual discussion of quality standards and that existing translation standards govern methods and procedures for achieving quality, rather than making normative statements on what constitutes a quality translation.

So our next task will be to propose a definition of a translation quality standard as distinct from other normative statements and concepts.

7.2. From norm to standard

We saw in 1.2 that the norm (or convention, in Nord's terminology) is akin to a linguistic or discourse instruction (or regularity) governing a specific problem (e.g., split infinitive) or discrete parameter (e.g., cohesion).

Several of the translation theorists with an interest in norms draw on the work of Renate Bartsch. She sees the norm as an explicit, codified rule expressing a notion of correctness and, in the language domain, making for efficient oral or written communication by removing, or reducing, complexity and contingency. Linguistic norms are norms of product, not of method or process, and are exemplified by *models* or *standards*, in the sense of forms to be imitated:

> ... norms consist of relationships between people, in which it is determined *what the model or standards which have to be followed are,*

> *who has to follow which models, who provides models, and who enforces, if necessary, adherence to the models. There are central models and less central models.* (Bartsch 1987: 70; my emphasis)

Specific linguistic norms may be morphosyntactic, phonological, semantic, and pragmatic, and are all subsumed under a single, broad highest-order norm expressing the need for effective communication (cf. Nord's "norm of functionality," 1.2):

> All specific linguistic norms are justified relative to the highest norm of communication, which is: "Express yourself in such a way that what you say is recognizable and interpretable by your partner in agreement with what you intend him to understand." (Bartsch 1987: 212)

For Bartsch, this "highest norm" is closely tied to the requirement of textual coherence and the purpose (illocutionary point) of discourse, which must be achieved (and preserved, for our purposes, in translation?) for communication to be effective.

The highest-order, general norm is an enduring one. Specific norms can be changed, however, as circumstances, society, and requirements evolve, as in stylistic norms (e.g., letter-writing styles), "which vanish with the disappearance of certain social relationships" (Bartsch 1987: 201).

Within the limits of the effective communication requirement, there is room for considerable variety and tolerance in a language community, Bartsch finds. As long as the highest general norm is observed, "functional deviation" from specific norms is tolerated: "[D]eviations are acceptable in communication under the restriction that we are able to count on the other's understanding the expressions as we do, i.e., on the other's being able to follow the deviation" (1987: 209). Thus she is able to conclude that acceptability in communication does not necessarily coincide with correctness of language use:

> Acceptability of appearance and use of expressions, therefore, is not simply identical with correctness with respect to valid specific linguistic norms; rather, it is correctness with respect to the highest norm. Correctness with regard to specific norms is only necessary as long as this serves correctness with respect to the principle of communication. What is correct with respect to this principle largely depends on the special demands of the particular situation of communication. In standard cases, correctness with respect to

> this highest norm is achieved by correctness with respect to specific linguistic norms. Cases in which this is not so justify deviance from specific linguistic norms and lead to change of linguistic norms, if these kinds of situation become important and occur regularly. (Bartsch 1987: 213)

Bartsch sees standard language as a codified selection of varieties of language items and, as such, a "central model" or "reference point" to be imitated by members of the language community. The same flexibility and tolerance of variety exists in what Bartsch calls the *empirical* standard, within the limits prescribed for effective communication. At the same time, a *normative,* prescriptive, codified standard is required to control variety and ensure that the language can meet the common communication expectations of the community.

But what is the *standard* language? It is a composite of all the specific linguistic norms accepted as part of the central model. In this sense, it mirrors the relationship between the translation quality standard, on the one hand, and the individual transfer and language parameters or criteria, on the other; conformity with those criteria means that the overall standard is observed.

We can use Bartsch's arguments to work toward a definition of the translation quality standard and a relevant rating grid.

7.3. Translation quality standard

The *Canadian Oxford Dictionary* defines the noun "standard" as follows:

> 1. an object or quality or measure serving as a basis or example or principle to which others conform or should conform or by which the accuracy or quality of others is judged (*present-day standards*).
> 2. a) the degree of excellence, etc. required for a purpose (*not up to standard*). b) average quality (*of a low standard*).
> 3. the ordinary procedure or quality or design of a product, without added or novel features.
>
> ...
>
> 7. a document specifying nationally or internationally agreed upon properties of manufactured goods, etc.
> 8. a thing recognized as a model for imitation, etc. (1998: 1415)

In respect of a translation quality standard, all five definitions are pertinent. In addition to the obvious concept of a standard of translation excellence, to be taken as a model and imitated, there is that of the document specifying accepted properties of products (definition 7) and procedures for ensuring quality (definition 3), as typified by ISO standards. Adapting the above definitions to the present study, we may say that the argumentation-centred TQA parameter grid developed here is a combination of procedural specifications and guidance on how to conduct TQA, while the rating grid elaborated in chapter six is in essence a product standard, serving to give a value to the translation as end product.

Bartsch gives us a theoretical basis for solving some other dilemmas of translation quality standardization, not the least of which are the notions of flexibility and tolerance and, concomitantly, that of acceptable deviation embraced by the standard. At the core of Bartsch's standard lies the highest-order norm of understandability and effective communication. If these requirements are met, even deviant utterances become acceptable under certain circumstances. In the same way, I have suggested that translations are adequate if the essential argument is accurately rendered, notwithstanding other weaknesses.

Another important notion is that of field- or use-specific norms. Similarly, the end use or area of specialization of a translation will dictate the application of specific parameters—I have already suggested style, usage and grammar, typography, and terminology as sets of norms, or parameters, to be applied in the case of translations for publication. In short, a flexible, comprehensive standard must include a number of "standard" grades. Note also that the required score for each parameter will be higher in the case of a translation for publication than in the case of one for information purposes only.

I therefore propose the following grade scheme, which also serves as a set of general and use-specific standards, in the sense of levels of quality to which professionals are expected to conform:

Publication standard

The text accurately renders all components of the argument schema and meets the requirements for all target-language parameters and other selected core and field- or use-specific parameters.

Information standard

The text accurately renders all components of the argument schema and meets requirements for selected core and field- or use-specific parameters.

MINIMUM STANDARD
The text accurately renders all components of the argument schema.

In fact, what I am defining here is the quality of the text exemplifying each standard or model—an exemplar, if you will. There is no single, universal standard here, such as "zero defects," but two specific standards to be applied according to context and text function (of course, "zero defects" could be a specific standard in itself or subsumed under a given standard). The approach is thus a modular one and could embrace other "grades" or standards. For example, if it were determined that correct terminology, not grammar, style, and usage, was the key parameter for certain scientific or technical texts, then the quality of the text exemplifying the "scientific/technical translation standard" would have to be defined accordingly.

We can make the definitions more precise by reintroducing a necessary component—that of the defect. We saw in chapter four that quality-control theorists defined critical and major defects in relation to safety, prevention of performance, and usability. Now that we have a theoretical basis for determining what constitutes the "essential message" of the text, we too can split the translation defect into critical and major categories and refine the definition of the major defect as presented in the microtextual models. We can describe the "critical" defect as one that entails failure to render an element of the argument or reasoning schema, since in our view such a defect materially reduces the usability of the translation. We can then reserve the term "major" for those defects involving a failure to render an important part of the microtext, but not of the superstructure or schema—in other words, the balance of the defects that would have been assessed as major under conventional microtextual models. We refine our definitions accordingly, adding a fourth grade to represent translations that meet none of the standards:

1. MAXIMUM/PUBLICATION STANDARD
The text renders all components of the argument schema and meets the requirements for all target-language parameters and other selected core and field/use-specific parameters. It contains no critical or major defects.

2. INFORMATION STANDARD
The text renders all components of the argument schema and meets requirements for selected core and field/use-specific parameters. It contains no critical defects.

3. Minimum standard

The text accurately renders all components of the argument schema. It contains no critical defects.

4. Substandard

The text fails to render the argument schema (contains at least one critical defect) and/or does not meet requirements for one or more core or field- or use-specific parameters.

The standards correspond to the "grades" proposed by Nord (see 1.1.2) in light of the varying functions of individual translations. Standard 1 (maximum/publication) corresponds to translations such as the popular criminology articles (texts 3 and 4) examined in chapter five, while standard 2 (information) corresponds to the statistical reports (texts 1 and 2). We use the word "minimum" for standard 3 in keeping with Wiggins's nomenclature (1993: 288), to represent a minimum acceptable performance "in the field." An evaluator might well apply the requirements of standard 3 to a translation for information purposes, depending on how important target-language quality was deemed to be.

Note that a translation will always be rated "substandard" if a component of the argument schema is inaccurately rendered. However, even a translation accurately rendering all argument schema components *may* be deemed "substandard" if it fails to meet one or more selected field- or use-specific requirements. In other words, it is "substandard" relative to the specific standard being required.

If there can be a *minimum* standard, there can also be a *maximum* one (Walton 1989: 276–77). The maximum standard is applicable not only to publications but also to translations such as ministerial speeches, which, while not for publication as such, may nonetheless require work of high quality. Thus the translations of texts 3 and 4 would meet the minimum professional standard but not the requirements of the maximum standard.

The evaluator is responsible for deciding, on the basis of his or her knowledge of the context (work statement, etc.), what standard is to be applied and selects an appropriate grid and weighting factors; the evaluator thus retains discretionary power. There is no discretion, however, as far as preservation of all elements of the argument schema is concerned.

We can now revisit the summary table of TQA results presented at the end of chapter five, and apply the proposed set of ARTRAQ standards.

Revised Summary Table of Assessments

Text	ARTRAQ Rating	Rationale
1 Statistical report	*Substandard*	Grounds mistranslated, in large part through failure to render conjunctives and thereby clarify propositional functions appropriately; therefore, argument schema not preserved in TT and critical defect present.
2 Statistical report	*Substandard*	Grounds, claims, narrative strategy misinterpreted; therefore, argument schema not preserved in TT and critical defects present.
3 Crime article	*Substandard*	Argument schema rendered. **Does not meet maximum/publication standard** because it does not meet publication quality criteria and contains major defects (based on ARTRAQ definition of major defect). **Note: Had the minimum standard been required, the translation would have met it.**
4 Crime article	*Substandard*	Argument schema rendered. **Does not meet maximum/publication standard** because it does not meet publication quality criteria and contains major defects (based on ARTRAQ definition of major defect). **Note: Had the minimum standard been required, the translation would have met it.**

CONCLUSION

I conclude with an assessment of ARTRAQ in light of the objectives set in chapter one.

1. TQA model

Under ARTRAQ, each unit of text, whether a word, a sentence, or a paragraph, is explicitly and necessarily related to macrotextual elements. Thus the mistranslation of an individual word, phrase, or sentence in the translation is not analyzed from the standpoint of degree of equivalence to the corresponding units in the source; it is judged according to the contribution that the ST unit makes to the purpose, or illocutionary point, of the text—a point made through the tools of argumentation, whatever the text type.

The argumentation parameters are thus macrotextual and microtextual at one and the same time. It is in this sense that my model responds to Bartsch's highest-order norm of communication and understandability, or text coherence, which is determined by macrostructure and schema (superstructure): "[T]he build-up of texts and their coherence are globally determined by the general theme, the 'macrostructure' of the text, and the kind of text, or 'superstructure'" (1987: 18–19). All the microtextual grammatical and semantic norms are validated by this higher-level requirement.

In addition, the refinement of the model enabled us to incorporate a more conventional, microtextual error analysis of various parameters as required by the nature of the text, client, or end use, and thus respond to the functional requirement of an assessment/evaluation system adaptable to different purposes and client needs. We can therefore say that the model already covers transfer of meanings at all levels and, through the extended, weighted variant, even offers the potential for a comprehensive set of parameters for target-language assessment as well.

In short, the prime advantage of ARTRAQ is that it is at once standards-referenced (fixed quality standards to be met) and criterion-referenced (varying quality criteria to be met depending on field or end use).

By applying Toulmin's argument schema to TQA, we have established a minimum level of acceptable quality and performance based on theory instead of convention, experience, and an arbitrary quantification of quality ratings. In answering the fundamental question of whether the TT accurately conveys the argument schema—that is, the core message—the evaluator proceeds according to very exacting criteria that leave little margin for variation and inconsistency between assessments (assuming consistency in evaluator competence).

If the translation deviates from the argument schema, it does not meet the minimum quality standard. This serves to counter the criticism of excessive subjectivity often levelled against evaluators and TQA systems and provides evaluators with a theory-based solution to the thorny problem of borderline cases.

Regarding the issue of graduating to an assessment of overall quality from a compartmentalized assessment of discrete parameters, assessment of core argumentation parameters covers most, if not all, elements of transfer. Building on that, the extended, modular ARTRAQ provides the flexibility needed to incorporate non-transfer and other field- or use-specific features. As such, the model fits the definition of an "aggregate measure" proposed by theorists of quality control: "A measurement can be aggregate if it represents a set of simple phenomena or a *combination of several measurements into one on the basis of a pre-established, preferably simple law*" (Fatzer and Stora 1990: 220; our translation).

The weighting of parameters has enabled us to generate an aggregate TQA without requiring too many calculations. Quantification does come into play in the weighting for parameters other than that of argument schema, but the intensive quantification of minor defects can be replaced by the evaluator's own judgment as to the importance of those parameters in the overall assessment. Note also that the passage from parameter analysis to aggregative, overall assessment is facilitated by the fact that ARTRAQ focuses on and gives weight to effectiveness of message transfer; it is not based on an unweighted mix of transfer and target-language parameters, as in the case of some conventional models.

It is the consistent recourse to argument schema analysis and the rating of translations on that basis that ensures reliability and stability over time. The evaluator has been given a precise framework and procedure for determining, not judging, what is essential in the ST. The model should therefore provide for greater reliability in assessment over time.

Validity is ensured by assessing parts of the text that contain key components of the argument schema. It is true that this does not necessarily make for efficiency. It may, however, obviate the need to assess the whole translation.

2. Definition of error

My goal was to develop a model in which error is defined, in terms of seriousness and/or quantity, in such a way that the overall judgment of the quality of the translation may be considered accurate beyond any reasonable doubt.

In the realm of modern quality control, Fatzer and Stora define "criticalité" as a key characteristic of a quality indicator:

> A critical measurement is one associated with a critical stage in a process; non-conformity in completing the stage means that the ultimate objective cannot be achieved. Any process or procedure can be broken down into a number of major subprocesses; the process and its major subprocesses are guided by means of a "dashboard," which is bound to include all the quality indicators: e.g., correct address on an invoice. (Fatzer and Stora, 1990: 220; our translation)

While the statement seems to focus on process rather than product, the example is indeed one of product, and of the type of criterion applied in TQA. Because of the theoretical underpinnings of the ARTRAQ model, which provides a clear definition of those elements in a process or product that are to be deemed major/critical, we now have a defensible definition of critical and major defect based on the notion of criticality—one that provides a stronger degree of validity for the overall judgment of the quality of a translation that do conventional microtextual approaches.

3. Definition of translation quality standard

Both the ARTRAQ model as a process or guiding standard and the rating grid as a product standard offer the theoretical basis and the flexibility required to meet most TQA needs and purposes. They provide the reliability, validity, comprehensiveness, and criticality required to resolve many of the conflicts that have raged over translation quality assessment.

The stumbling block to acceptance and adoption of translation quality standards over the years has, in my view, been the failure to justify quantitative standards and assessments with reference to the highest norm of understandability, effective communication, and, by extension, text usability. In other words, the criticisms levelled at texts deemed unsatisfactory were not justified with respect to the norm of communication. The introduction of a new minimum standard, the avoidance of solely quantitative tolerance levels, and the redefinition of the major defect in terms of what is essential *to the text as a whole* lend the model a new flexibility that could help resolve some of the conflicts of the past.

Robert Larose concluded that a comprehensive translation quality assessment model was in all likelihood impossible to design. I hope that by shifting the focus of assessment from lexical and syntactic items to text, message, and argument, I have offered, if not a comprehensive alternative, at least an approach that covers all the significant elements in instrumental translation and places emphasis on quality according to translation function and end use.

APPENDIX ONE

MODEL ASSESSMENT

To give the reader a comprehensive picture of the results of an ARTRAQ assessment, I show how an evaluator might mark up the translation of the passage and complete the grids for text 2 (see 5.2.1).

> TARGET TEXT
>
> (Para. 3) The advantage of the previous *(T—mistranslation)* project is that it provides estimates for the distance travelled that fluctuate with the years instead of being considered constant values, as it *(L—usage)* seems to be the case currently with this model. However, the data is not available according to the exact age of the vehicles, but rather according to age groups: 2 years and under, 3-5 years, 6-8 years, 9 years and over. The possibility, by using Bayesian analysis tools developed by Ms Nathalie Boucher, *(L—syntax)* of producing series equivalent to ***(T—critical defect: grounds of argument schema misconstrued)*** the provincial or regional scale (Maritimes, Quebec, Ontario, Prairies, British Columbia) should be studied for the next agreement.
>
> (Para. 4) In its review of input variables, the OEE indicates that the CVS (1999–) could constitute a new source of data for this variable. The survey is supposed, in effect (*T—mistranslation*), to be an important source of data for estimating distance travelled. We ***(T—major defect bordering on critical: author's narrative strategy misconstrued, undermining force of grounds and claim)*** note that the survey covers more than the requirements *(T—mistranslation)* for the present variable and consequently is also assumed to be a good source for the variable estHTrkPVDT (Estimated Heavy Truck per Vehicle Distance Travelled). The CVS survey was designed to estimate distances travelled by *(T—omission)* various categories of road vehicles, including light, medium and heavy trucks. In the

travel log book for light vehicles (cars and trucks), we ***(T—narrative strategy defect repeated)*** asked our ***(defect repeated)*** respondent to specify vehicle use for each trip (question 7 of the 2000 version) and one of the uses on the list refers to work use ("Driving as part of the job"). Distance estimates for light trucks can therefore be segmented according to the type of use (personal or commercial), making it possible to specifically *(L—redundant)* target commercial distance for the purposes of the present *(L—usage)* variable. The log book for higher mass *(L—terminology)* trucks (medium and heavy), used by default for commercial purposes, also shows the distance travelled for each of the vehicles selected for each of their trips, during the survey period. The two weight categories of the vehicles retained *(L—gallicism)* for sample stratification, 10 000-33 000 lbs and over 33 000 lbs, then make it possible to produce separate estimates for medium trucks (present variable) and heavy trucks (variable estHTrkPVDT). An estimate of the total commercial distance for each of the two categories of trucks can thus be obtained.

ARTRAQ Grid

Core Parameters

Element	**Translation assessment**
Argument schema	Grounds and claim inaccurately rendered
Propositional functions/ conjunctives/other inference indicators	Accurately rendered overall
Arguments	Accurately rendered overall
Narrative strategy	Inaccurately rendered

Since the translation is for information purposes, the evaluator will apply the information standard.

The above grid summarizes the results of the evaluator's work in assessing how well the translator has preserved the content and structure of the argumentation features in ST. This part of the ARTRAQ process will have served to identify most, if not all, weaknesses in transfer of message. In selecting parameters for the weighted ARTRAQ grid, the evaluator will take into account the fact that the subject is specialized and based on scientific logic and that the translation is primarily for information purposes. Accordingly, the completed grid might look like this:

Weighted ARTRAQ Grid

Parameter	Weight (/10)	Minimum Requirement	Quality (/10)	Rationale	Score (/100)
Argument schema	3	(10) 30	0	Misinterpretation of schema elements	0
Propositional functions/ conjunctives/ other inference indicators	2	(8) 16	8	One error	16
Narrative strategy	2	(6) 12	0	Narrative strategy misconstrued	0
Typography	1	(6) 6	10	No errors	10
Terminology	2	(8) 16	8	One error	16
Total	10	**80**			**42%**

Given the weightings assigned to the various parameters, a score of 80% (30% for argument schema and 50% for selected parameters) would constitute the minimum requirement for this translation to meet the information standard. In the end, the evaluator finds it to be substandard on two counts: (1) failure to preserve the argument schema fully (sufficient in itself to warrant a substandard rating), and (2) failure to preserve the narrative strategy.

Narrative Rating

Grade	Description	Translation Rating
Maximum/ publication standard	The text accurately renders all components of the argument schema and meets the requirements for all target-language parameters and other selected core and field- or use-specific parameters. It contains no critical or major defects.	
Information standard	The text accurately renders all components of the argument schema and meets requirements for selected core and field- or use-specific parameters. It contains no critical defects.	
Minimum standard	The text accurately renders all components of the argument schema. It contains no critical defects.	
Substandard	The text fails to render the argument schema (contains at least one critical defect) and/or does not meet requirements for one or more core or field- or use-specific parameters.	X

For practical purposes, the evaluator can boil the three grids down to one, as shown below.

Weighted ARTRAQ Grid

Parameter	Weight (/10)	Minimum Requirement	Quality (/10)	Rationale	Score (/100)
Argument schema	3	(10) 30	0	Misinterpretation of schema elements	0
Propositional functions/ conjunctives/ other inference indicators	2	(8) 16	8	One error	16
Narrative strategy	2	(6) 12	0	Narrative strategy misconstrued	0
Typography	1	(6) 6	10	No errors	10
Terminology	2	(8) 16	8	One error	16
Total	10	**80**			**42%**
Grade	**Substandard**				

APPENDIX TWO

TERMINOLOGY

Here are some important terms related to TQA, argumentation theory, educational assessment and evaluation, and quality standards. An italicized term in a definition is one that is itself defined in this appendix.

Acceptability (in translation) *Quality* of translation in relation to *norms* originating in the target culture (Toury 1981: 53–69).

Adequacy (in translation) *Quality* of a translation as compared to the *source text*. An adequate translation is a translation that realizes in the *target language* the textual relationships of a source text with no breach of its own basic linguistic system (Toury 1981: 53–69).

Argument Creation of, and provision of support for, a thesis, idea, request, or statement.

Assessment See **Evaluation (in translation)**.

Authentic (test, in educational assessment) Faithfully representing the contexts facing workers in a field of study or the real-life "tests" of adult life, involving tasks that are either replicas of or analogous to the kinds of problems faced by adult citizens or consumers or professionals in the field, requiring the student to produce a *quality* product and/or performance, and marked on the basis of transparent or demystified criteria and *standards* (Wiggins 1993: 229).

Backing Overarching principle, law, or value governing and justifying the relationship between *grounds* and *claim* in argumentative discourse (Toulmin et al. 1984: 25ff).

Claim (discovery) Conclusion of an argument; the main point toward which all other elements of an argument converge (Toulmin et al. 1984: 25ff).

Coherence Property of a text or utterance created by the logical, semantic, and syntactic interdependence of its constituent elements. In contrast to *cohesion*, which relates to language, coherence relates to conceptual interrelatedness within the *text* (Delisle et al. 1999: 124).

Continuity of the meaning of a *text* from one idea to another and plausibility of such meaning (Brunette 2000: 175).

Cohesion Linguistic property of a *text* or utterance created by grammatical and linking words used to connect words within a sentence or sentences with each other (Delisle et al. 1999: 124).

Context Non-linguistic circumstances surrounding the production of the *discourse* to be assessed. For assessors of general or pragmatic texts, these circumstances include the end user of the *target text* (in its relation to that of the *source text*), the position of the end user, the author, the time and place in which the translation will be used, the life span of the translated text, the text type, the medium used to disseminate the *text*, the social situation (e.g., multilingualism) and ideological circumstances (e.g., political) surrounding production of the *target text* (Brunette 2000: 178–79).

Convention Non-statutory *norm*, which need not be enacted, formulated, or promulgated (Ullmann-Margalit 1977: 97).

Co-text The *text* to which a sample is attached.

Criterion-referenced assessment A type of measure that does not compare individuals within a specific population but measures achievement against specific, distinguishable criteria (Harper et al. 1999: 22).

Defect Failure to meet a usability requirement or reasonable expectation. In translation, text-level error adversely affecting usability of a translation and, in an argumentation-centred TQA context, reflecting misinterpretation of the argument schema.

Dialogical Involving the development of argument and ideas through dialogue or the confrontation of perspectives.

Discourse A connected series of utterances or a *text* (Delisle et al. 1999: 135).

Ethos Moral image conveyed of writer/speaker in a text/speech and effect of that image on the reader/listener (Declerq 1993: 47).

Evaluation (in translation) Placing of a value on a translation—that is, awarding a mark (McAleester 2000: 231). Determination of the *quality* of a translation or a check after the fact for management purposes. A *rating* is assigned (Brunette 2000, 173).

Formative assessment Monitoring learning and giving continuous feedback on student's progress.

Frame Prototypical situation, background, environment, or *context* in which events and actions may occur (van Dijk 1980: 233).

Generalizability Degree to which information collected in an *assessment* can be expanded to a wider domain. For example, if a student does well on one translation test, can one conclude accurately that the student "knows how to translate"? Since individuals usually cannot be assessed on a whole domain, samples of performance provide the basis for generalizability (Harper et al. 1999: 54).

Grade (in translation) Label or rank that can be assigned to a translation to indicate that it meets specific *quality requirements*. The term indicates an acknowledgment that there are different levels of acceptable quality. Thus a "low-grade" translation may be of satisfactory quality.

Grounds Information, matters of common knowledge, well-known truisms, or commonsense observations presented in support of an argument (Toulmin et al. 1984: 25ff).

Illocutionary point Basic purpose of writer/speaker making an utterance.

Inference indicator Word or phrase serving to indicate that one statement is being given as a reason for another (Thomas 1986: 12–13).

Instrumental translation *Text* designed for utilitarian communication, of generally immediate, short-term use, which imparts some information of a nature that is general or specific to a domain, and for which aesthetics play a very secondary role (Delisle et al. 1999: 169). For the purposes of this study, excludes translation of literature, religious works, and philosophy. Also known as "pragmatic translation."

Language error An error that occurs in the *target text* and can be ascribed to a lack of knowledge of the *target language* or of its use (Delisle et al. 1999: 150).

Macrostructure Structure of content, or definition, of larger part, or whole, of *discourse* based on meanings of individual *propositions* and of the connections between them; part of discourse that represents larger part, or whole, of discourse, such as title, subtitle, or summary.

Macrotext *Text* structure larger than the sentence, such as the paragraph, section, and chapter.

Measurement (in translation) Systematic activity or activities designed to quantify quality of translation.

Metadiscourse Reference, within the *text,* to the act and *context* of writing or arguing (Williams 1990: 40).

Microtext Graphic, phonemic, morphosyntactic, and lexical (subsentence/sentence) elements of discourse.

Modalizer See **Qualifier**.

Norm Prescribed guide for conduct or action which is generally complied with by members of the group concerned (Ullman-Margalit 1977: 12)

Norm-referenced assessment Type of measure that is "normed" or compares individuals within a specific population. It measures differences between the individuals being assessed (Harper et al. 1999: 22).

Pathos Mode of persuasion entailing appeal to emotions of readership or audience.

Perlocutionary point Intended effect or result of writer/speaker making an utterance.

Proposition Sentence or clause containing a statement (or question) about the world and usually linked logically to one or more other sentences or clauses.

Qualifier Linguistic element that enhances or mitigates the force of an argument (Toulmin et al. 1984: 25ff). Synonym: **Modalizer**.

Quality (in translation) Degree to which a translation meets established or implicit requirements or a *standard*.

Quality assurance (in translation) Systematic pre-delivery activity or activities designed to give assurance that a translation meets *quality* requirements.

Quality control (in translation) Verification to ensure that the product to be delivered or already delivered complies with requirements, language norms and established criteria, with the ultimate goal of saving time and resources. The quality control of a translation can range from a partial monolingual reading to a bilingual reading of samples (Brunette 2000: 173).

Quality requirements (in translation) Characteristics or attributes of a translation required by client and/or end user.

Rating Symbolic representation of, or descriptive label or numerical value for, a level of *quality*.

Rebuttal (restriction) Statement of exceptional circumstances that contradicts or may undermine the force of an argument (Toulmin et al. 1984: 25ff).

Reliability Extent to which an assessment produces the same results when repeatedly administered to the same population under the same conditions (Harper et al. 1999: 51).

A TQA system is reliable if the evaluator's decisions are consistent and if the assessment/evaluation criteria are stable. Verification of reliability would involve a search for defects in the *measurement* procedures themselves, defects that could lead to biases or undue variations in TQA findings over a period of time. For TQA purposes, are procedures in place to ensure that the evaluators do not fluctuate between excessive rigour and extreme flexibility? Are requirements for *quality* clearly enough defined for decisions on borderline cases to be made with consistency and ample justification? Is the TQA expert always objective? (M. Williams 1989: 15).

Schema Overall categorical structure of *discourse,* such as narrative or argumentative schema (van Dijk 1980: 233). Synonym: **Superstructure**.

Script Prototypical episode—that is,, sequence of events and actions taking place in a *frame*. Scripts are typically based on different types of *conventions* (habits, rules, laws, etc.), which say which actions should or could be accomplished where and when and in what order (van Dijk 1980: 234).

Skopostheorie (scopos theory) Theory of translation based on the idea that it is the scopos (i.e., purpose or scope) of the translated *text* that determines the translation process (Nord 1991a: 93).

Source language The language from which a translation is made (Delisle et al. 1999: 180).

Source text The *text* on which a translation is based (Delisle et al. 1999: 181).

Stability Ability of measuring instrument to maintain constant its measurement characteristics with time.

Standard A document, established by consensus and approved by a recognized body, that provides for common and repeated use; rules, guidelines, or characteristics for activities or their results, aimed at the achievement of the optimum degree of order in a given *context* (Delisle et al. 1999: 182).

Standards-referenced assessment (in education) Version of *criterion-referenced assessment,* in which there is less emphasis on the specification and analysis involved in describing and assessing criteria for performance. It relies on verbal descriptions and exemplars (typical of designated levels of performance) to help specify standards that designate levels of *quality* in performance (Harper et al. 1999: 22).

Summative assessment/evaluation (in education) Action taken at the end of a period of instruction to provide information about student's progress and achievement, and often resulting in the assigning of a grade.

Superstructure See **Schema**.

Target language The language in which the *text* is written (Delisle et al. 1999: 184).

Target text Any *text* that is the product of translation activity (Delisle et al. 1999: 185).

Teleological assessment Determination of *quality* with reference to the consequences, outcomes, or goals of the subject of the *assessment*.

Text A written document of variable length that constitutes a whole when viewed from a semantic perspective (Delisle et al. 1999: 187).

Thematic string Sequence of conceptually related words in a text (Williams 1990: 84).

Translation error Any fault occurring in the *target text*, ascribable either to ignorance or to inadequate application of translation principles, rules, or procedures, and resulting from the misinterpretation of a *source text* segment or methodological error (Delisle et al. 1999: 189).

Translation norm Behavioural regularity accepted (in a given community) as being a model or standard of desired translation behaviour. Notion of what constitutes correct or appropriate behaviour in translation (Chesterman 1993: 4–5).

Trope Figure of speech involving deviation from the ordinary and principal signification of a word or group of words (Corbett and Connors 1999: 379).

Validity In education, the extent to which an *assessment* measures what it is designed to measure. There are several types of assessment validity, including the following:

> *Construct validity*—whether the assessment adequately measures the underlying skill (construct) being measured

Concurrent validity—whether the assessment gives substantially the same results as does another test of the same skill
Content validity—whether an assessment covers the skills necessary for performance—for example, whether the content of a translation test is an appropriate sample of the content of the course
Predictive validity—whether an assessment accurately predicts future performance (Harper et al. 1999: 49).

In translation, validity refers to the degree to which TQA findings permit inferences about the target population (the whole text or a corpus). TQA validity is the extent to which the translation samples evaluated are representative of the whole translation, the translator, or the service, and the degree to which the evaluator is then able to make judgments about the level of *quality*, the strong points and the weak points of the entity concerned on the basis of those samples (M. Williams 1989: 16). For purposes of translation teaching, the construct validity (adequate measurement of underlying skills) and predictive validity (adequate measure of future performance) of the proposed model will be of particular interest.

Warrant Statement indicating how the information and observations in the grounds of an argument are connected to the *claim* or conclusion (Toulmin et al. 1984: 25ff).

BIBLIOGRAPHY

Adab, Beverly. 2000. Evaluating Translation Competence. In Christina Schäffner and Beverly Adab, eds., *Developing Translation Competence* (Philadelphia: John Benjamins), 215–28.

Andrews, Richard. 1995. *Teaching and Learning Argument*. London: Cassell.

Angenot, Marc. 1982. *La parole pamphlétaire*. Paris: Payot.

Antaki, Charles. 1994. *Explaining and Arguing: The Social Organization of Accounts*. London: Sage Publications.

Bartsch, Renate. 1987. *Norms of Language: Theoretical and Practical Aspects*. London: Longman.

Bensoussan, Marsha, and Judith Rosenhouse. 1990. Evaluating Students' Translations by Discourse Analysis. *Babel*, 65–84.

Berman, Antoine. 1995. *Pour une critique des traductions: John Donne*. Paris: Éditions Gallimard.

Billig, Michael. 1996. *Arguing and Thinking: A Rhetorical Approach to Social Psychology*. 2nd edition. Cambridge: Cambridge University Press.

Brunette, Louise. 2000. Towards a Terminology for Translation Quality Assessment. *The Translator*, 6 (2): 169–82.

Canadian Oxford Dictionary. Toronto: Oxford University Press, 1998.

Chesterman, Andrew. 1993. From "Is" to "Ought": Laws, Norms and Strategies in Translation Studies. *Target*, 5 (1): 1–20.

——. 1997. *Memes of Translation: The Spread of Ideas in Translation Theory*. Amsterdam: John Benjamins.

Circuit. 1994. La qualité totale: Engagez-vous, qu'y disaient! No. 44.

Corbett, Edward, and Robert Connors. 1999. *Classical Rhetoric for the Modern Student*. New York: Oxford University Press.

Council of Translators and Interpreters of Canada. 2001. *CTIC Standard Certification Translation Examination: Marker's Guide—Official Languages*. Ottawa.

Crystal, David, and Derek Davy. 1969. *Investigating English Style*. Harlow: Longman.

Darbelnet, Jean. 1977. Niveaux de la traduction. *Babel*, 23 (1): 6–17.

Declerq, Gilles. 1993. *L'Art d'argumenter: Structures rhétoriques et littéraires.* Brussels: Éditions universitaires.

Delisle, Jean, et al., eds. 1999. *Translation Terminology.* Philadelphia: John Benjamins.

Dubois, Jean, et al. 1970. *Rhétorique générale.* Paris: Larousse.

Engineering Society for Advanced Mobility in Land, Sea, Air and Space. 2000. SAE J2450 Translation Quality Metric Task Force. L'Étalon de qualité.

Fatzer, Georges, and Gilbert Stora. 1990. La mesure de la qualité. In Vincent Laboucheix, ed. *Traité de la qualité totale.* Paris: Dunod, 217–24.

Gaskell, Philip. 2000. Standard Written English. *English Today,* 16 (1): 48–52.

Greimas, A. J. 1983. *Du sens: Essais sémiotiques.* 2 vols. Paris: Seuil.

Gross, Alan G. 1991. Rhetoric of Science Without Constraints. *Rhetorica,* 9 (4): 283–99.

Gouadec, Daniel. 1989. *Le traducteur, la traduction et l'entreprise.* Paris: Afnor.

Halliday, M. A. K. 1978. *Language as Social Semiotic: The Social Interpretation of Language and Meaning.* Baltimore: University Park Press.

Halliday, M. A. K., and Ruqaiya Hasan. 1976. *Cohesion in English.* London: Longman.

Harper, Mark, Ken O'Connor, and Marilyn Simpson. 1999. *Quality Assessment: Fitting the Pieces Together.* Toronto: OSSTF.

Hatim, Basil, and Ian Mason. 1997. *The Translator as Communicator.* London: Routledge.

Hayes, G., and H. Romig. 1982. *Modern Quality Control.* Encino, Calif.: Glencoe Publishing Co.

Hönig, Hans. 1998. Positions, Power and Practice: Functionalist Approaches and Translation Quality Assessment. In Christina Schäffner, ed. 1998. *Translation and Norms* (Toronto: Multilingual Matters), 6–34.

Horguelin, Paul. 1978. *Pratique de la révision.* Montreal: Linguatech.

House, Juliane. 1997. *Translation Quality Assessment: A Model Revisited.* Tübingen: Gunter Narr Verlag.

Institut für Angewandte Linguistik und Translatologie. 1999. TQ2000: Internationale Fachtagung Translationsqualität. Universität Leipzig, 28–30 October. www.uni-leipzig.de/~ialt/tq2000.htm

Ishikawa, K. 1985. *What is Total Quality Control? The Japanese Way.* Englewood Hills, N.J.: Prentice-Hall.

Language International. 1998. Quality: The Struggle over Translation Standards. 10(5).

Larose, Robert. 1987. *Théories contemporaines de la traduction.* Sillery: Presses de l'Université du Québec.

——. 1994. Qualité et efficacité en traduction: réponse à F. W. Sixel. *Meta,* 34 (2): 362–73.

——. 1998. Méthodologie de l'évaluation des traductions. *Meta*, 43 (2): 163–86.

McAleester, Gerard. 2000. The Evaluation of Translation into a Foreign Language. In Christina Schäffner and Beverly Adab, eds., *Developing Translation Competence* (Philadelphia: John Benjamins), 229–42.

McCloskey, Donald N. 1985. *The Rhetoric of Economics*. Madison: University of Wisconsin Press.

McGuire, J. E., and T. Melia. 1989. Some Cautionary Strictures on the Writing of the Rhetoric of Science. *Rhetorica*, 7 (1): 87–99.

——. 1991. The Rhetoric of the Radical Rhetoric of Science. *Rhetorica*, 9 (4): 301–16.

Mendenhall, Vance. 1990. *Une introduction à l'analyse du discours argumentatif*. Ottawa: Presses de l'Université d'Ottawa.

Myerson, George, and Yvonne Rydin. 1996. *The Language of Environment: A New Rhetoric*. London: UCL Press.

Nord, Christiane. 1991a. Scopos, Loyalty, and Translational Conventions. *Target*, 3 (1): 91–109.

——. 1991b. *Text Analysis in Translation: Theory, Methodology, and Didactic Application of a Model for Translation-Oriented Text Analysis*. Amsterdam and Atlanta: Rodopi.

——. 1992. Text Analysis in Translator Training. In Cay Dollerup and Anne Loddegard, eds., *Teaching Translation and Interpreting* (Amsterdam: John Benjamins), 39–48.

Ontario. Government Translation Services. 2000. Evaluation Procedures. 5th Draft. Toronto.

Ouellet, Pierre. 1984. La désénonciation: les instances de la subjectivité dans le discours scientifique. *Protée*, 18 (2): 43–53.

——. 1985. La vision des choses: la focalisation dans le discours scientifique. *Protée*, 19 (1): 33–45.

——. 1992. *Voir et savoir: La perception des univers du discours*. Montreal: Éditions Balzac.

Perelman, Chaïm. 1977. *L'empire rhétorique: rhétorique et argumentation*. Paris: Vrin.

Perelman, Chaïm, and Lucie Olbrechts-Tyteca. 1969. *The New Rhetoric: A Treatise on Argumentation*. Translated by J. Wilkinson and P. Weaver. Notre Dame, Ind.: University of Notre Dame Press.

Reiss, Katharina. 1981. Type, Kind and Individuality of Text: Decision Making in Translation. *Poetics Today*, 2 (4): 121–31.

Reiss, Katharina, and Hans Vermeer. 1984. *Grundlegung einer allgemeinen Translationstheorie*, Tübingen: Niemeyer.

Roulet, E., et al. 1985. *L'articulation du discours en français contemporain*. Berne: Peter Lang.

Ryan, Eugene E. 1984. *Aristotle's Theory of Rhetorical Argumentation*. Montreal: Les Éditions Bellarmin.

Rybacki, K. C. 1996. *Advocacy and Opposition. An Introduction to Argumentation*. Toronto: Allyn and Bacon.

Saragossi, Maggy. 1991. *Persuasion et séduction: Le discours politico-commercial du Canada sur l'Amérique latine*. Montréal: Éditions Balzac.

Searle, John. 1969. *Speech Acts: An Essay on the Philosophy of Language*. Cambridge: Cambridge University Press.

Société française des traducteurs. 2003. La norme pas à pas. http://www.sft.fr/membres/norme3.html

Sturz, Wolfgang. 1998. DIN 2345 Hits the Language Industry. *Language International* 10 (5): 18–19, 41.

Thomas, Stephen Naylor. 1986. *Practical Reasoning and Natural Language*. Englewood Hills, Calif.: Prentice-Hall.

Toulmin, Stephen, Richard Rieke, and Allan Janik. 1984. *An Introduction to Reasoning*. 2nd ed. New York: Macmillan.

Toury, Gideon. 1981. Translated Literature: System, Norm, Performance: Toward a TT-Oriented Approach to Literary Translation. *Poetics Today*, 2 (4): 9–27.

——. 1994. *Descriptive Translation Studies and Beyond*. Amsterdam: John Benjamins.

——. 1999. A Handful of Paragraphs on "Translation" and "Norms." in Translation Studies. In Christina Schäffner, ed. 1999. *Translation and Norms* (Toronto: Multilingual Matters), 9–31.

Ullmann-Margalit, Edna. 1977. *The Emergence of Norms*. Oxford: Clarendon Press.

van Dijk, Teun. 1980. *Macrostructures. An Interdisciplinary Study of Global Structures in Discourse. Interaction and Cognition*. Hillsdale, N.J.: Lawrence Erlbaum Assoc.

van Leuven-Zwart, Kitty. 1990. Shifts in Meaning in Translation: Do's and Don't's? In Marcel Thelen and Barbara Lewandowska-Tomaszczyk, eds. *Translation and Meaning*, 1 (Maastricht: Rijkshogeschool), 226–33.

Vignaux, Georges. 1976. *L'Argumentation: essai d'une logique discursive*. Geneva: Droz.

——. 1988. *Le discours acteur du monde: Énonciation, argumentation et cognition*. Gap: Ophrys.

Walton, Douglas. 1989. *Informal Logic*. Cambridge: Cambridge University Press.

Widdowson, H. G. 1978. *Explorations in Applied Linguistics*. Oxford: Oxford University Press.

Wiggins, Grant. 1993. *Assessing Student Performance: Exploring the Purpose and Limits of Testing*. San Francisco: Jossey-Bass Publishers.

Williams, Joseph. 1990. *Style: Toward Clarity and Grace*, Chicago: Chicago University Press.

Williams, Malcolm. 1989. Creating Credibility out of Chaos: The Assessment of Translation Quality. *TTR*, 2 (2): 13–33.

FURTHER READING

1. TQA models and translation quality standards

Canada. Translation Bureau. 1978. *La traduction au service de l'état et du pays. Doctrine, conception générale et méthode*. Ottawa.

Canada. Translation Bureau. 1986. Quality Standards. *Management News*, 9: 4

Canada. Translation Bureau. Translation Operations Branch. 1990. *Strategies 1991–94. Toward 1994: The Challenge of Quality*. Hull, Quebec.

Canada. Translation Bureau.Terminology and Linguistic Services Directorate. 1993. *Contrôle de la qualité des traductions. Cahier d'information*. Hull, Quebec.

Canada. Translation Bureau. Professional and Technical Training Directorate. 1994. *Pleins feux sur la qualité: Rapport sur les tendances en 1993–1994*. Hull, Quebec.

Council of Translators and Interpreters of Canada. 1994. Comité de révision de l'examen d'agrément en traduction. *Rapport final*. Hull, Quebec.

Fan, Shouyi. 1990. A Statistical Method for Translation Quality Assessment. *Target*, 2 (1): 43–67.

Gouadec, Daniel. N.d. Présentation du Système d'évaluation positive des traductions (SEPT). Translation Bureau. Hull, Quebec.

Gouadec, Daniel. 1981. Paramètres d'évaluation des traductions. *Meta*, 26 (2): 99–115.

Gouadec, Daniel. 1989. Comprendre, évaluer, prévenir: Pratique, enseignement et recherche face à l'erreur et à la faute en traduction. *TTR*, 2 (2): 35–54.

Gouadec, Daniel. 1989. *Le traducteur, la traduction et l'entreprise*. Paris: Afnor.

House, Juliane. 1977. *A Model for Translation Quality Assessment*. Tübingen: Gunter Narr Verlag.

Newmark, Peter. 1988. *A Textbook of Translation*. Toronto: Prentice Hall.

Nida, Eugene, and Charles Taber. 1969. *The Theory and Practice of Translation*. Leiden: E. J. Brill.

Reiss, Katharina. 2000. *Translation Criticism—The Potential and Limitations*.

Translated by Errol F. Rhodes. Manchester: St. Jerome Publishing.
Williams, Malcolm. 2001. Application of Argumentation Theory to Translation Quality Assessment. *Meta*, 46 (2): 326–44.

2. Documentation and research on norms, standards, quality control and management

Chomsky, Noam. 1980. *Rules and Representations*. New York: Columbia University Press.
Dyson, Steve. 1994. "Horses for Courses" or Meeting Customer Needs, Both Implicit and Explicit. In Catriona Picken, ed., *Quality—Assurance, Management and Control*. Proceedings of the Seventh Annual Conference of the Institute of Translation and Interpreting, April 28–29, 1994, Nottingham, U.K. (London: Institute of Translation and Interpreting), 87–94.
Gordon, John. 1994. A Quality Standard for Translations. In Catriona Picken, ed., *Quality—Assurance, Management and Control*. Proceedings of the Seventh Annual Conference of the Institute of Translation and Interpreting, April 28–29, 1994, Nottingham, U.K. (London: Institute of Translation and Interpreting), 34–41.
Hermans, Theo. 1991. Translation Norms and Correct Translations. In Kitty van Leuven-Zwart and Ton Naaijkens, eds., *Translation Studies: The State of the Art*. Proceedings of the First James S. Holmes Symposium on Translation Studies. Amsterdam and Atlanta: Rodopi, 155–69.
Hermans, Theo. 1999. Translation and Normativity. In Christina Schäffner, ed., *Translation and Norms* (Toronto: Multilingual Matters), 50–71.
International Organization for Standardization. 1996a. *ISO Standards Compendium: ISO 9000 Quality Management*. 6th edition. Geneva.
International Organization for Standardization. 1996b. *ISO 9000-1. Quality Management and Quality Assurance Standards*. Geneva.
Laboucheix, Vincent, ed. 1990. *Traité de la qualité totale*. Paris: Bordas.
Lewis, David K. 1969. *Convention: A Philosophical Study*. Cambridge, Mass.: Harvard University Press.
Picken, Catriona, ed. 1994. *Quality—Assurance, Management and Control*. Proceedings of the Seventh Annual Conference of the Institute of Translation and Interpreting, April 28–29, 1994, Nottingham, U.K. London: Institute of Translation and Interpreting.
Rose, Marilyn Gaddis. 1981. Translation Types and Conventions. In Marilyn Gaddis Rose, ed., *Translation Spectrum: Essays in Theory and Practice* (Albany: SUNY), 31–40.

Rose, Marilyn Gaddis, ed. 1981. *Translation Spectrum: Essays in Theory and Practice*. Albany: SUNY, 1981.

Samuelsson-Brown, Geoffrey. 1996. Working Procedures, Quality and Quality Assurance. In Rachel Owens, ed. *The Translator's Handbook*. 3rd ed. (London: Aslib), 103–35.

Schäffner, Christina, ed. 1999. *Translation and Norms*. Toronto: Multilingual Matters.

United Nations. Headquarters. 1993. Quality Control in the Working Environment of International Organizations. Unpublished paper. New York.

United Nations. United Nations Industrial Development Organization. 1993. The Translation Process. Translation/Revision: Quantity versus Quality Standards. Unpublished paper. Geneva.

Urmson, J. O. 1965. On Grading. Flew, Anthony, ed. *Logic and Language*. Garden City, N.Y.: Doubleday, 379–409.

Viaggio, Sergio. 1999. The Limitations of a Strictly Socio-Historical Description of Norms: A Response to Theo Hermans and Gideon Toury. In Christina Schäffner, ed., *Translation and Norms* (Toronto: Multilingual Matters), 122–28.

Wright, Georg Henrik von. 1963. *Norm and Action*. London: Routledge and Kegan Paul.

3. Educational assessment

Martinez Melis, Nicole. 1997. Évaluation et traduction: cadre de recherche sur l'évaluation dans la didactique de la traduction. Thesis. Universitat Autònoma de Barcelona.

Martinez Melis, Nicole, and Amparo Hurtado. 2001. Assessment in Translation Studies: Research Needs. *Meta*, 46 (2): 272–87.

4. Discourse analysis, argumentation theory, speech act theory, theory of linguistics, theory of meaning

Accardo, Alain, and Philippe Corcuff. 1986. *La sociologie de Bourdieu. Textes choisis et commentés*. 2nd ed. Bordeaux: Le Mascaret.

Aristotle. 2001. *The Basic Works of Aristotle*. Edited by Richard McKeon. New York: Modern Library.

Barthes, Roland. 1966. Introduction à l'analyse structurale des récits. *Communications*, 8: 1–27.

Barthes, Roland. 1967. Le discours de l'histoire. *Social Science Information*, 6 (4): 65–75.

Benveniste, Émile. 1966. *Problèmes de linguistique générale*. Paris: Gallimard.

Benveniste, Émile. 1969. Sémiologie de la langue. *Semiotica*, 1–12.

Bruce, Donald. 1995. *De l'intertextualité à l'interdiscursivité*. Toronto: Paratexte.

Chatman, Seymour. 1969. New Ways of Analyzing Narrative Structure, With an Example From Joyce's *Dubliners*. *Language and Style*, 2 (1): 4–45.

De Beaugrande, Robert. 1980. *Text, Discourse and Process: Toward a Multidisciplinary Science of Texts*. Norwood, N.J.: Ablex.

De Beaugrande, Robert, and Wolfgang Dressler. 1981. *Introduction to Text Linguistics*. London: Longman.

Dolezel, Lubomír. 1971. Toward a Structural Theory of Content in Prose Fiction. In Seymour Chatman, ed., *Literary Style: A Symposium* (London: Oxford University Press), 95–110.

Dolezel, Lubomír. 1976. Narrative Worlds. In Ladislav Matejka, ed., *Sound, Sign and Meaning: Quinquagenary of the Prague Linguistic Circle* (Ann Arbor: University of Michigan), 542–52.

Ducrot, Oswald. 1972. Preface to John Searle, *Les Actes de langage*. Paris: Hermann.

Ducrot, Oswald. 1980. *Les échelles argumentatives*. Paris: Éditions de Minuit.

Ducrot, Oswald, and Tzvetan Todorov. 1972. *Dictionnaire encyclopédique des sciences du langage*. Paris: Seuil.

Dupriez, Bernard. 1980. *Gradus: Les procédés littéraires*. Paris: Union générale d'édition.

Dupriez, Bernard. 1991. *A Dictionary of Literary Devices. Gradus, A–Z*. Translated and adapted by Albert Halsall. Toronto: University of Toronto Press.

Eco, Umberto. 1992. *Les limites de l'interprétation*. Translated by Myriem Bouzaher. Paris: Grasset.

Esprit, 12 (December 1974). Lecture I: L'espace du texte.

Esprit, 11 (November 1975).

Esprit, 1 (January 1976). Lecture II: Le texte dans l'espace.

Foucault, Michel. 1969. Qu'est-ce qu'un auteur? *Bulletin de la Société française de philosophie*, 64: 73–104.

Greimas, A. J. 1966. *Sémantique structurale*. Paris: Larousse.

Greimas, A. J., and E. Landowski. 1979. *Introduction à l'analyse du discours en sciences sociales*. Paris: Hachette.

Grimshaw, Jane. 1990. *Argument Structure*. Cambridge, Mass.: MIT Press.

Halloran, Michael, and Annette Norris Bradford. 1984. Figures of Speech in the Rhetoric of Science and Technology. In Robert J. Connors, Lisa S. Ede, and Andrea A. Lunsford, eds., *Essays on Classical Rhetoric and Modern*

Discourse (Carbondale: Southern Illinois University Press), 179–92.

Halsall, Albert W. 1988. *L'art de convaincre: Le récit pragmatique, rhétorique, idéologie, propagande*. Toronto: Paratexte.

Iser, Wolfgang. 1978. *The Act of Reading: A Theory of Aesthetic Response*. Baltimore: Johns Hopkins University Press.

Itkonen, Esa. 1983. *Causality in Linguistic Theory: A Critical Investigation Into the Philosophical and Methodological Foundations of "Non-Autonomous" Linguistics*. Bloomington: Indiana University Press.

Kuhn, Deanna. 1991. *The Skills of Argument*. Cambridge: Cambridge University Press.

Leith, Dick. 1994. The Rhetor's Guide. *Rhetorica*, 12 (2): 211–26.

Macherey, Pierre. 1966. *Pour une théorie de la production littéraire*. Paris: François Maspero.

Maingueneau, Dominique. 1976. *Initiation aux méthodes de l'analyse du discours: problèmes et perspectives*. Paris: Hachette.

Maingueneau, Dominique. 1984. *Genèses du discours*. Brussels: Pierre Mardaga.

Molinié, Georges. 1992. *Dictionnaire de rhétorique*. Paris: Librairie générale française.

Nanni, Luciano. 1991. Art et critique: la liberté en tant que pertinence. *Cahiers Ferdinand de Saussure*, 45: 249–60.

Nanni, Luciano. 1994. *I cosmi, il metodo: diario d'arte e di epistemologia 1979/89*. Bologna: Book Editore.

Nanni, Luciano. 1995. L'arte? L'estetica va bene, ma la scienza che c'entra? In Stefano Zecchi, ed., *Estetica. Le arti e la scienze* (Bologna: Il Mulino), 153–76.

Nanni, Luciano. 1996. Estetica e semiotica: il 'ribaltone' post-strutturalista. *Parol*, 12: 26–39.

Perelman, Chaïm. 1977. *L'empire rhétorique: rhétorique et argumentation*. Paris: Vrin.

Rastier, François. 1987. *Sémantique interprétative*. Paris: Presses universitaires de France.

Rastier, François. 1989. *Sens et textualité*. Paris: Hachette Supérieur.

Reboul, Anne, and Jacques Moeschler. 1998a. *La pragmatique aujourd'hui. Une nouvelle science de la communication*. Paris: Seuil.

Reboul, Anne, and Jacques Moeschler. 1998b. *Pragmatique du discours. De l'interprétation de l'énoncé à l'interprétation du discours*. Paris: Armand Colin.

Récanati, François. 1981. *Les énoncés performatifs*. Paris: Les Éditions de Minuit.

Ricoeur, Paul. 1975. *La métaphore vive*. Paris: Seuil.

Ricoeur, Paul. 1986. *Du texte à l'action: Essais d'herméneutique, II*. Paris: Seuil.

Russell, D. A., and M. Winterbottom, eds. 1972. *Ancient Literary Criticism: The*

Principal Texts in New Translations. London: Oxford University Press.

Rybacki, K. C. 1996. *Advocacy and Opposition. An Introduction to Argumentation*. Toronto: Allyn and Bacon.

Schrag, Calvin. 1992. *The Resources of Rationality*. Bloomington: Indiana University Press.

Searle, John. 1979. *Expression and Meaning: Studies in the Theory of Speech Acts*. Cambridge: Cambridge University Press.

Searle, John, and Daniel Vanderveken. 1985. *Foundations of Illocutionary Logic*. Cambridge: Cambridge University Press.

Souchard, Maryse. 1989. Le phénomène d'argumentation dans un discours de presse. *Texte*, 8–9: 219–26.

Stati, Sorin. 1989. Isotopy, Coreference, and Redundancy. In Maria-Elisabeth Conti, ed., *Text and Discourse Connectedeness*. Proceedings of the Conference on Connexity and Coherence. Urbino (Italy), July 1984 (Amsterdam: John Benjamins), 207–22.

Todorov, Christo. 1971. La hiérarchie des liens dans le récit. *Semiotica*, 3 (2): 121–39.

Todorov, Tzvetan. 1969. *Grammaire du Décaméron*. Paris: Mouton.

Todorov, Tzvetan. 1970. Les transformations narratives. *Poétique*, 3: 322–33.

Toulmin, Stephen. 1964. *The Uses of Argument*. Cambridge: Cambridge University Press.

van Dijk, Teun. 1997. *Text and Context. Explorations in the Semantics and Pragmatics of Discourse*. London: Longman.

van Dijk, Teun, and Walter Kintsch. 1983. *Strategies of Discourse Comprehension*. Toronto: Academic Press.

Walton, Douglas. 1990. *Practical Reasoning: Goal-Driven, Knowledge-Based, Action-Guiding Argumentation*. Savage, Md.: Rowman and Littleford.

5. Research on translation quality, the translation unit, and error analysis

Ahulu, Samuel. 1997. The Evaluation of Errors and 21st-century Structure and Usage. *English Today*, 50: 33–39.

Brislin, Richard. 1976. *Translation: Applications and Research*. New York: Gardner Press.

Campbell, Stuart. 1999. A Cognitive Approach to Source Text Difficulty in Translation. *Target*, 11 (1): 33–63.

Cary, E., and R. W. Jumpelt, eds. 1963. *Quality in Translation*. Proceedings of the 3rd Congress of the International Federation of Translators, Bad Godesberg, 1959. New York: Pergamon Press.

Dancette, Jeanne. 1989. La faute de sens en traduction. *TTR*, 2, (2): 83–102.

De Beaugrande, Robert. 1978. *Factors in a Theory of Poetic Translating*. Assen: Van Gorcum.

Donaher, Paul. 1994. Evaluating Quality (1). In Catriona Picken, ed., *Quality—Assurance, Management and Control*. Proceedings of the Seventh Annual Conference of the Institute of Translation and Interpreting, April 28–29, 1994, Nottingham, U.K. (London: Institute of Translation and Interpreting), 76–80.

Ekundayo, Simpson. 1975. Methodology in Translation Criticism. *Meta*, 20 (4): 251–62.

Ekundayo, Simpson. 1978. Translation and Value Judgment. *Meta*, 23, (3): 211–19.

Even-Zohar, Itamar. 1986. The Textemic Status of Signs in a Literary Text and Its Translation. *Poetics Today*, 11 (1): 629–33.

Graham, J. D. 1994. Evaluating Quality (2). In Catriona Picken, ed., *Quality—Assurance, Management and Control*. Proceedings of the Seventh Annual Conference of the Institute of Translation and Interpreting, April 28–29, 1994, Nottingham, U.K. (London: Institute of Translation and Interpreting), 81–86.

Kingscott, Geoffrey. 1996. Providing Quality and Value. In Rachel Owens, ed., *The Translator's Handbook*. 3rd ed. (London: Aslib), 137–46.

Koller, Werner. 1995. The Concept of Equivalence and the Object of Translation Studies. *Target*, 7 (2): 191–222.

Lewis, Philip E. 1985. The Measure of Translation Effects. In Joseph F. Graham, ed., *Difference in Translation* (Ithaca: Cornell University Press), 31–62.

Maier, Carol, ed. 2000. *Evaluation and Translation*. Special issue of *The Translator*, 6 (2).

Mossop, Brian. 1989. Objective Translational Error and the Cultural Norm of Translation. *TTR*, 2 (2): 55–72.

Neubert, Albrecht. 2000. Competence in Language, in Languages, and in Translation. In Christina Schäffner and Beverly Adab, eds., *Developing Translation Competence* (Philadelphia: John Benjamins), 3–18.

Nord, Christiane. 1992. The Relationship Between Text Function and Meaning. In Marcel Thelen and Barbara Lewandowska-Tomaszczyk, eds., *Translation and Meaning* (Maastricht: Rijkshogeschool), vol. 2, 91–96.

Nord, Christiane. 1996. El error en la traducción: Categoriás y evaluación. In Amparo Hurtado Albir, ed., *La enseñanza* (Castelló: Universitta Jaumé 1), 91–107.

Ratcliffe, Paul. 1994. Quality: Absolutism or Pragmatism? In Catriona Picken, ed., *Quality—Assurance, Management and Control*. Proceedings of the Seventh Annual Conference of the Institute of Translation and Interpreting, April 28–29, 1994, Nottingham, U.K. (London: Institute of Translation and Interpreting), 47–55.

Reiss, Katharina. 1983. Quality in Translation. *Babel*, 29: 198–208.
Sager, Juan. 1989. Quality and Standards—The Evaluation of Translations. In Catriona Picken, ed. , *The Translator's Handbook*. 2nd ed. (London: Aslib), 91–102.
Schäffner, Christina. 1998. *Translation and Quality*. Toronto: Multilingual Matters.
Schäffner, Christina. 2000. Running Before Walking? Designing a Translation Programme at Undergraduate Level. In Christina Schäffner and Beverly Adab, eds., *Developing Translation Competence* (Philadelphia: John Benjamins), 143–56.
Schäffner, Christina, and Beverly Adab, eds. 2000. *Developing Translation Competence*. Philadelphia: John Benjamins.
Simpkin, Richard E. 1983. Translation Specifications. In Catriona Picken, ed., *The Translator's Handbook*. (London: Aslib), 129–39.
TTR, 2 (2). 1989. L'erreur en traduction. Edited by Robert Larose.
Université de Montréal. 2001. Evaluation: Parameters, Methods, Pedagogical Aspects / Évaluation: paramètres, méthodes, aspects pédagogiques. Special issue of *Meta*, 46 (2): 326–44.

6. Translation studies

Baker, Mona. 1992. *In Other Words: A Coursebook on Translation*. New York: Routledge.
Berman, Antoine. 1984. *L'épreuve de l'étranger*. Paris: Gallimard.
Chevalier, Jean-Pierre, and Marie-France Delport. 1995. *Problèmes linguistiques de la traduction: l'horlogerie de Saint Jérôme*. Paris: L'Harmattan.
Choul, Jean-Claude. 1985. Une théorie de la traduction est-elle nécessaire? *Texte*, 4: 137–50.
Curtis, Sheryl. 1998. Visible Hands: Inferring Translation Strategy. Ph.D. thesis. Concordia University, Montreal.
Even-Zohar, Itamar. 1981. Translation Theory Today: A Call for Transfer Theory. *Poetics Today*, 2 (4): 1–7.
Gutknecht, Christoph, and Lutz J. Rolle. 1996. *Translating by Factors*. Albany: SUNY Press.
Gutt, Ernst-August. 1991. *Translation and Relevance: Cognition and Context*. Oxford: Basil Blackwell.
Graham, Joseph F., ed. 1985. *Difference in Translation*. Ithaca: Cornell University Press.
Hewson, Lance, and Jacky Martin. 1991. *Redefining Translation: The Variational Approach*. New York: Routledge.

Lörscher, Wolfgang. 1991. *Translation Performance, Translation Process, and Translation Strategies. A Psycholinguistic Investigation.* Tubingen: Gunter Narr Verlag.

Mel'cuk, Igor. 1978. Théorie de langage, théorie de traduction. *Meta,* 23 (4): 271–302.

Neubert, Albrecht, and Gregory Shreve. 1992. *Translation as Text.* Kent, Ohio: Kent University State Press.

Owens, Rachel, ed. 1996. *The Translator's Handbook.* 3rd ed. London: Aslib.

Picken, Catriona, ed. 1989. *The Translator's Handbook.* 2nd ed. London: Aslib.

Riffaterre, Michael. 1985. Transposing Presuppositions on the Semiotics of Literary Translation. *Texte,* 4: 99–109.

Ross, Stephen David. 1981. Translation and Similarity. In Marilyn Gaddis Rose, ed. *Translation Spectrum: Essays in Theory and Practice* (Albany: SUNY), 8–22.

Snell-Hornby, Mary. 1995. *Translation Studies: An Integrated Approach.* Revised ed. Amsterdam: John Benjamins.

Steiner, George. 1992. *After Babel: Aspects of Language and Translation.* 2nd ed. Oxford: Oxford University Press.

Toury, Gideon. 1990. What Are Descriptive Studies into Translation Likely to Yield Apart From Isolated Descriptions? In Kitty van Leuven-Zwart and Ton Naaijkens, eds., *Translation Studies: The State of the Art.* Proceedings of the First James S. Holmes Symposium on Translation Studies (Amsterdam and Atlanta: Rodopi), 179–92.

AUTHOR AND SUBJECT INDEX